The Observer's Pocket Series

AIRCRAFT

The Observer's Book of

AIRCRAFT

COMPILED BY
WILLIAM GREEN

WITH SILHOUETTES BY
DENNIS PUNNETT

DESCRIBING 139 AIRCRAFT
WITH 245 ILLUSTRATIONS

1979 EDITION

FREDERICK WARNE

LIBRARY OF CONGRESS CATALOG CARD NO: 57 4425

ISBN 0 7232 1591 X

Printed in Great Britain

INTRODUCTION TO THE 1979 EDITION

With this, the twenty-eighth annual edition of *The Observer's Book of Aircraft*, we approach the end of yet another decade, and it is instructive to compare this volume with that issued at the end of the *last* decade. A comparison reveals that the ratio between military and civil aircraft entries remains virtually unchanged, although the variety of types within certain categories (e.g. business executive transports and basic-advanced jet trainers) has altered dramatically, and marginally less than two score of the types to be found on the pages of the 1969 edition remain in one form or another in this edition ten years later. But what of the hundred plus aircraft types included then and omitted now? Barely more than a dozen are no longer flying and some of the remainder are today numerically among the most common types to be seen; such aircraft as the Boeing 707, the Trident, the DC-8, the Skyhawk and the Sukhoi Su-7, to mention but a few. To some readers unfamiliar with *The Observer's Book of Aircraft*, the exclusion of such important aircraft types is apparently difficult to understand. Therefore, in this, the last edition of the decade, it is perhaps appropriate to reiterate the *raison d'être* of this annual publication.

The Observer's Book of Aircraft, unlike most contemporary source books which devote themselves primarily to those aeroplanes most likely to be seen, concentrates on the recent variants of those aircraft currently in production, under test at the time of closing for press, or scheduled to commence their test programmes during the volume's year of currency. With each successive edition, the data provided for aircraft that reappear are updated and the accompanying three-view silhouette drawings carefully checked to cater for any modifications or changes that may have been applied to the aircraft concerned. *The Observer's Book* thus provides a continuous record of aircraft design development in all the principal categories.

This year's edition includes a variety of new military aircraft that commenced their flight test programmes during the course of the twelve months past, such as the F-18 Hornet, the Sea Harrier and AV-8B derivatives of the V/STOL Harrier, the Mirage 2000 and the Fouga 90, and these are joined by the Super Mirage 4000 and ADV Tornado scheduled to commence flight testing this year. Business executive transport types have continued to proliferate, with the Mitsubishi MU-300 and Canadair Challenger that appeared last year being joined this by such newcomers and derivative types as the Foxjet, the Citation III and the Gulfstream III, and several new helicopters appear on the following pages for the first time, together with new variants of a number of established aircraft types. For those aircraft that the reader is most likely to *see*, the companion *Observer's Basic Aircraft Directories* are recommended.

WILLIAM GREEN

AERITALIA G.222L

Country of Origin: Italy.

Type: General-purpose military transport.

Power Plant: Two 5,060 shp Rolls-Royce Tyne RTy 20 (Mk. 801) turboprops.

Performance: Max. cruising speed (at 54,013 lb/24 500 kg), 350 mph (563 km/h) at 20,000 ft (6 095 m); max. range (with 11,023-lb/5 000-kg payload), 1,740 mls (2 800 km), (with 16,535-lb/7 500-kg payload), 870 mls (1 400 km), (with overload payload of 19,840 lb/9 000 kg), 435 mls (700 km); ferry range, 3,175 mls (5 110 km); initial climb (at 61,729 lb/28 000 kg), 2,050 ft/min (10,4 m/sec).

Weights: Operational empty, 37,919 lb (17 200 kg); max. take-off, 61,730 lb (28 000 kg).

Accommodation: Flight crew of three—four and 48 fully-equipped troops, 36 paratroops, 36 casualty stretchers plus four seated wounded/medical attendants, three 105 mm howitzers, or two light trucks or jeep-type vehicles.

Status: Prototype G.222L (34th production G.222) to fly autumn 1979, with deliveries against initial order for 20 (from Libya) to commence late 1980, when production rate will be one per month.

Notes: The G.222L is a re-engined version of the standard G.222 (see 1978 edition) for the Libyan Arab Republic Air Force, Tynes replacing the General Electric T64s. First of two G.222 prototypes flown July 18, 1970, and 44 of standard model ordered by Italian Air Force with delivery tempo of one per two months at beginning of 1979. An electric counter-measures adaptation of the 12th production G.222 is illustrated above.

AERITALIA G.222L

Dimensions: Span, 94 ft 2 in (28,70 m); length, 74 ft 5½ in (22,70 m); height, 32 ft 1¾ in (9,80 m); wing area, 882·64 sq ft (82,00 m²).

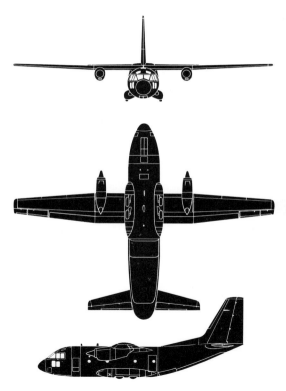

AERITALIA/PARTENAVIA P.68T

Country of Origin: Italy.

Type: Light multi-role utility and transport aircraft.

Power Plant: Two 330 shp (derated from 420 hp) Allison 250-B17B turboprops.

Performance: (At 4,850 lb/2 200 kg) Max. speed, 216 mph (348 km/h) at sea level to 10,000 ft (3 280 m), 238 mph (383 km/h) at 20,000 ft (6 095 m) or Mach 0·34; range cruise, 205 mph (330 km/h) at 10,000 ft (3,280 m); initial climb, 2,600 ft/min (13,2 m/sec); service ceiling, 25,000 ft (7 620 m).

Weights: Empty, 3,020 lb (1 370 kg). Max. take-off, 5,291 lb (2 400 kg).

Accommodation: Seating for six in three side-by-side pairs with dual controls for front pair for light transport or business executive roles and provision for armament system for military roles with four 400-lb (181-kg) capacity wing hardpoints and two 250-lb (113-kg) capacity fuselage hardpoints for rocket launchers or pods, supply containers, bombs, etc.

Status: Prototype P.68T first flown on September 11, 1978.

Notes: Derived from the piston-engined P.68R Victor (see 1978 edition) by Aeritalia in collaboration with the Partenavia company, the P.68T embodies some structural strengthening, a marginally longer fuselage, enlarged vertical tail surfaces and extended wing auxiliary tanks. It is intended for application in a wide variety of civil and military roles, the latter including armed reconnaissance and patrol, and close support. The Italian Air Force possesses a requirement for an aircraft in this category.

AERITALIA/PARTENAVIA P.68T

Dimensions: Span, 39 ft 4½ in (12,00 m); length, 31 ft 11¾ in (9,74 m); height, 11 ft 9⅛ in (3,58 m); wing area, 200·2 sq ft (18,60 m²).

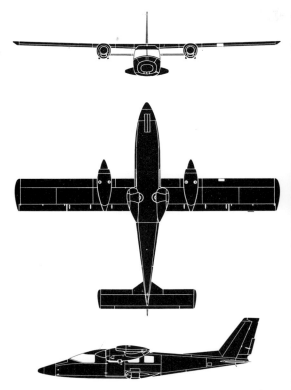

AERMACCHI MB 339

Country of Origin: Italy.

Type: Two-seat basic and advanced trainer.

Power Plant: One 4,000 lb (1 814 kg) Fiat-built Rolls-Royce Viper 632-43 turbojet.

Performance: Max. speed (clean configuration), 558 mph (898 km/h) at sea level, 508 mph (817 km/h) at 30,000 ft (9 145 m) or Mach 0·77; max. range (clean configuration), 1,094 mls (1 760 km), (ferry configuration with two 143 Imp gal/650 l pylon tanks), 1,310 mls (2 110 km); initial climb, 6,600 ft/min (33,5 m/sec); service ceiling, 47,500 ft (14 630 m).

Weights: Empty equipped, 6,883 lb (3 125 kg); loaded (clean), 9,700 lb (4 400 kg); max. take-off, 13,000 lb (5 897 kg).

Armament: For armament training and light strike roles a maximum of 4,000 lb (1 815 kg) may be distributed between six underwing stations, the inner and mid stations being of 750 kg (340 kg) capacity and the outer stations being of 500 lb (230 kg) capacity.

Status: Two prototypes flown on August 12, 1976, and May 20, 1977, respectively, and first of six pre-series aircraft flown on July 20, 1978. Initial batch of 15 aircraft (including pre-series machines) being built at beginning of 1979 against total Italian Air Force requirement of approximately 100 aircraft.

Notes: Based on the airframe of the earlier MB 326 and incorporating the strengthened structure of the MB 326K, the MB 339 incorporates an entirely redesigned forward fuselage providing vertically staggered seats for pupil and instructor. Photo-reconnaissance equipment or armament pod may be inserted in bay beneath rear seat.

AERMACCHI MB 339

Dimensions: Span, 35 ft 7 in (10,86 m); length, 36 ft 0 in (10,97 m); height, 13 ft 1 in (3,99 m); wing area, 207·74 sq ft (19,30 m²).

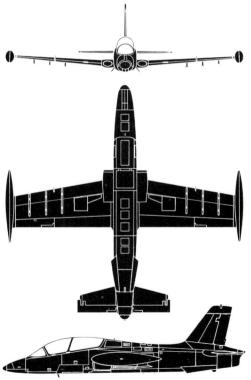

AÉROSPATIALE FOUGA 90

Country of Origin: France.
Type: Tandem two-seat basic trainer.
Power Plant: Two 1,543 lb (700 kg) Turboméca Astafan IIG turbofans.
Performance: (Estimated) Max. speed, 404 mph (650 km/h) at 24,605 ft (7 500 m); max. continuous cruise, 373 mph (600 km/h); range at optimum altitude, 888 mls (1 430 km), (with two 27·5 Imp gal/125 l wingtip tanks), 1,305 mls (2 100 km); initial climb, 1,870 ft/min (9,5 m/sec).
Weights: Empty equipped, 5,733 lb (2 600 kg); loaded (flying training mission), 7,716 lb (3 500 kg); max. take-off, 8,157 lb (3 700 kg).
Armament: For armament training or light attack roles two 7,62-mm guns and four 110-lb (50-kg) or 275-lb (125-kg) bombs, two 110-lb (50-kg) bombs and two 18×68-mm rocket pods, or two AS 11 or AS 12 ASMs and two 7,62-mm gun pods.
Status: Prototype first flown on August 20, 1978.
Notes: Developed as a private-venture low-cost aircraft, the Fouga 90 retains essentially similar wings and tail of the CM 170 Magister trainer and the undercarriage of the CM 175 mated with a new fuselage incorporating vertically-staggered ejection seats, pressurisation and turbofan engines. Although no orders for the Fouga 90 had been announced by the beginning of 1979, it is claimed to offer the lowest initial and operating costs of any turbofan-powered trainer.

AÉROSPATIALE FOUGA 90

Dimensions: Span, 39 ft 2⅘ in (11,96 m); length, 33 ft 10¾ in (10,33 m); height, 9 ft 2¼ in (2,80 m); wing area, 197·84 sq ft (18,38 m²).

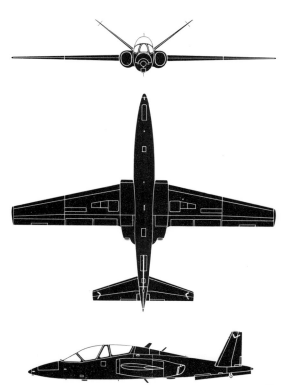

AÉROSPATIALE (SOCATA) TB-30

Country of Origin: France.
Type: Tandem two-seat primary-basic trainer.
Power Plant: One 300 hp Avco Lycoming IO-540-K six-cylinder horizontally-opposed engine.
Performance: (Estimated) Max. cruise, 219 mph (352 km/h) at sea level; max. range, 746 mls (1 200 km); initial climb, 1,500 ft/min (7,62 m/sec); service ceiling 15,000+ ft (4 600+ m); max endurance, 3 hrs at 5,000 ft (1 525 m).
Weights: Max. take-off, 2,645 lb.
Status: The TB-30 has been designed to meet an *Armée de l'air* requirement and the prototype is scheduled to commence its flight test programme in September 1979. Series production is intended to be undertaken by the SOCATA subsidiary of Aérospatiale.
Notes: Evolved to the so-called *Epsilon* programme for a trainer to be introduced between the CAP 10 and Magister in the *Armée de l'Air* training syllabus, the TB-30 will be suitable for the initiation of blind flying, VFR and IFR navigation, and initiation in aerobatics.

14

AÉROSPATIALE (SOCATA) TB-30

Dimensions: Span, 24 ft 3 in (7,40 m); length, 24 ft 3 in (7,40 m); height, 8 ft 10 in (2,70 m); wing area, 96·87 sq ft 9,00 m²).

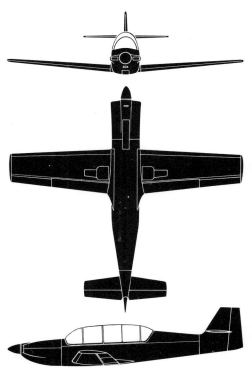

AIRBUS A300B4-100

Country of Origin: International consortium.

Type: Medium-haul commercial transport.

Power Plant: (A300B4-101) Two 51,000 lb (23 130 kg) General Electric CF6-50C turbofans.

Performance: Max. cruise, 578 mph (930 km/h) at 28,000 ft (9 185 m); econ. cruise, 540 mph (869 km/h) at 31,000 ft (9 450 m); long-range cruise, 521 mph (839 km/h) at 33,000 ft (10 060 m); range (with max. payload, no reserve), 2,618 mls (4 213 km); max. range (with 48, 350-lb/21 932-kg payload), 3,994 mls (6 428 km).

Weights: Operational empty, 194,130 lb (85 060 kg); max. take-off, 347,200 lb (157 500 kg).

Accommodation: Crew of three on flight deck with provision for two-man operation. Seating for 220–336 passengers in main cabin in six-, seven- or eight-abreast layouts.

Status: First and second A300Bs flown October 28,1972, and February 5, 1973 (B1 standard), respectively, with third (to B2 standard) flying on June 28, 1973. First A300B4 flown December 26, 1974, and 59 (all versions) delivered by beginning of 1979, when production rate was two per month against firm orders for 123 (plus 53 options). Production to increase to three per month by year's end.

Notes: The A300B is manufactured by a consortium of Aérospatiale, British Aerospace and Deutsche Airbus. The A300B2-100 is the basic version, the A300B2-200 having Krueger flaps for improved field performance, and the A300B4-100 is a longer-range model with the Krueger flaps and a centre-section fuel tank, the A300B4-200 having increased gross weight (363,800 lb/165 000 kg). The A300C4 is a convertible passenger/freight variant and the A310 is a short-fuselage, rewinged derivative scheduled to fly in 1981 with service entry in 1983.

AIRBUS A300B4-100

Dimensions: Span, 147 ft 1¼ in (44,84 m) : length, 175 ft 11 in (53,62 m) ; height, 54 ft 2 in (16,53 m) ; wing area, 2,799 sq ft (260,00 m²).

17

ANTONOV AN-28 (CASH)

Country of Origin: USSR.

Type: Light STOL general-purpose transport and feederliner.

Power Plant: Two 960 shp Glushenkov TVD-10A turbo-props.

Performance: Max. continuous cruising speed, 217 mph (350 km/h); range (with 3,415-lb/1 550-kg payload), 620 mls (1 000 km), (with max. fuel), 805 mls (1 300 km); initial climb rate, 2,360 ft/min (11,99 m/sec).

Weights: Normal loaded, 12,785 lb (5 800 kg); max. take-off, 13,450 lb (6 100 kg).

Accommodation: Flight crew of one or two and up to 18 passengers in high-density configuration, but standard configuration for 15 passengers in three-abreast seating (one to port and two to starboard), the seats folding back against the cabin walls when the aircraft is employed in the freighter or mixed passenger/freight roles. Alternative versions provide for six or seven passengers in an executive transport arrangement and an aeromedical version accommodates six stretchers and a medical attendant.

Status: Initial prototype flown as An-14M in September 1969. A production prototype was tested early in 1974 with 810 hp Isotov TVD-850 turborprops, the aircraft having meanwhile been redesignated An-28, and this was re-engined with Glushenkov TVD-10A engines with which it first flew in April 1975. Series production was not initiated until late 1978, with service entry scheduled for 1980, and licence production is to take place in Poland.

Notes: The An-28 has undergone protracted development, but the initiation of production as a successor to the An-2 biplane in some roles was finally announced in 1978.

ANTONOV AN-28 (CASH)

Dimensions: Span, 72 ft $2\frac{1}{8}$ in (22,00 m); length, 42 ft $6\frac{7}{8}$ in (12,98 m); height, 15 ft 1 in (4,60 m).

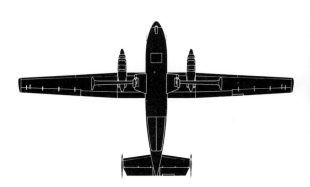

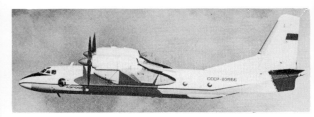

ANTONOV AN-32 (CLINE)

Country of Origin: USSR.

Type: Commercial freighter and military tactical transport.

Power Plant: Two 4,190 ehp Ivchenko A1-20M turboprops.

Performance: Max. continuous cruise, 317 mph (510 km/h) at 26,250 ft (8 000 m); range (with 13,215-lb/6 000-kg payload and 45 min reserve), 500 mls (800 km), (max. fuel), 1,370 mls (2 200 km); service ceiling, 31,150 ft (9 500 m).

Weights: Max. take-off, 57,270 lb (26 000 kg).

Accommodation: Flight crew of five and 39 passengers on tip-up seats along fuselage sides, 30 fully-equipped paratroops or 24 casualty stretchers and one medical attendant.

Status: Flown in prototype form late 1976, the An-32 is expected to enter service with both Aeroflot and the Soviet Air Force from 1979–80.

Notes: The An-32 is the latest development in the An-24 (*Coke*) series of transport aircraft and is intended specifically for operation under hot-and-high conditions. Based on the An-26 (*Curl*) and possessing an essentially similar airframe with combined rear-loading ramp/supply drop door, but featuring a 33% increase in available power, the An-32 is capable of operating from unpaved runways and features a 4,400-lb (2 000-kg) capacity electric hoist and a conveyor in the fuselage to assist in the loading of heavy freight. Obvious differences to the An-26 include the overwing engine installation, enlarged ventral fins, upper wing spoilers and dog-tooth wing leading edges. The military version of the An-26 has been widely exported and it is believed that development of the An-32 is largely the result of shortcomings displayed by the earlier aircraft in operations under conditions of very high temperatures or from high-altitude airfields. The An-32 has been offered to several air forces (including that of India).

ANTONOV AN-32 (CLINE)

Dimensions: Span, 95 ft 9½ in (29,20 m); length, 78 ft 1 in (23,80 m); height, 28 ft 1½ in (8,58 m); wing area, 807·1 sq ft (74,98 m²).

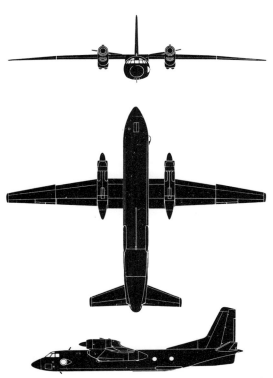

ANTONOV AN-72

Country of Origin: USSR.

Type: STOL tactical transport.

Power Plant: Two 14,500 lb (6 575 kg) Lotarev turbofans.

Performances: (Estimated) Max. cruising speed, 435 mph (700 km/h); max. continuous cruise, 373 mph (600 km/h); tactical radius (with 11,000-lb/5 000-kg payload), 435 mls (700 km).

Weights: (Estimated) Max. take-off (STO), 50,000 lb (22 680 kg); max. overload, 65,000 lb (29 485 kg).

Accommodation: Flight crew likely to comprise four or five members and it is probable that 40 fully-equipped troops may be carried, alternative loads possibly including 30–36 para-troops or some 25 casualty stretchers.

Status: The prototype An-72 was flown on December 22, 1977, and it was assumed that an evaluation programme was continuing at the beginning of 1979. It is improbable that the An-72 will enter Soviet Air Force service before 1982–83.

Notes: The An-72, remarkably similar in concept to the Boeing YC-14 (see 1978 edition) advanced technology transport evolved to meet the requirements of the USAF's AMST (Advanced Military STOL Transport) programme, utilises the upper-surface-blowing concept, the USB being provided by engine exhaust gases flowing over the upper wing surfaces and associated flap system. Although the prototype An-72 displays Aeroflot markings, the aircraft is apparently intended primarily for military roles, but is likely to be used also on commercial freight services to remote airstrips inaccessible to more conventional transport aircraft. The accompanying general arrangement silhouette should be considered as provisional.

ANTONOV AN-72

Dimensions: No detail available for publication.

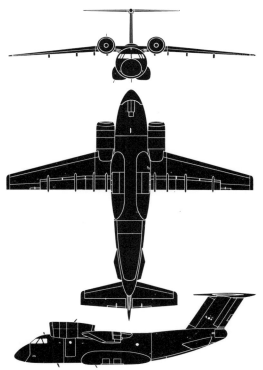

BAe ONE-ELEVEN 670

Country of Origin: United Kingdom.
Type: Short- to medium-range commercial transport.
Power Plant: Two 12,550 lb (5 698 kg) Rolls-Royce Spey 512-14DW turbofans.
Performance: Max. cruising speed, 550 mph (885 km/h) at 21,000 ft (6 400 m); range (with max. payload), 1,440 mls (2 316 km) at 528 mph (850 km/h) at 30,000 ft (9 150 m); initial climb, 3,000 ft/min (15,2 m/sec).
Weights: Typical operational empty, 51,482 lb (23 351 kg); max. take-off (standard), 84,000 lb (38 102 kg), (with centre section tank), 92,000 lb (41 731 kg).
Accommodation: Flight crew of two and typical single-class layout for 79 passengers, with max. of 89 passengers.
Status: Prototype One-Eleven 670 (conversion of Series 400 aircraft) scheduled to commence testing with all proposed features in April 1979, with customer deliveries offered for 1980. Initial production run of 215 One-Elevens completed early 1975, and production resumed in following year with initial batch of 10 of which first flown December 20, 1976. Production of further 20 authorised by beginning of 1979, when orders totalled 227 and further 82 to be licence-manufactured in Romania (22 being delivered as kits during 1980–85, and six to be produced annually thereafter until 1995).
Notes: The One-Eleven 670 is a derivative of the 475 (see 1978 edition) with new wing leading-edge fillets, an advanced anti-skid system, automatic braking and lift dumping, and a new engine exhaust ejector silencer, this combination offering improved field performance and lower noise levels. The features of the 670, individually or collectively, may be applied to the longer-bodied Series 500 (see 1970 edition) which will then become the Series 600.

BAe ONE-ELEVEN 670

Dimensions: Span, 93 ft 6 in (28,50 m); length, 93 ft 6 in (28,50 m); height, 24 ft 6 in (7,47 m); wing area, 1,031 sq ft (95,78 m²).

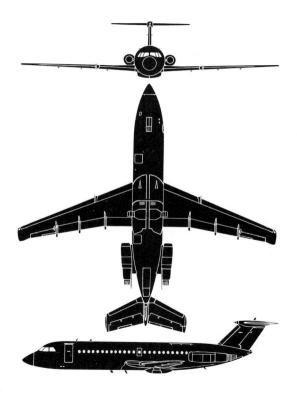

BAe COASTGUARDER

Country of Origin: United Kingdom.
Type: Medium-range maritime patrol and surveillance aircraft.
Power Plant: Two 2,280 ehp Rolls-Royce Dart RDa 7 Mk. 535-2 turboprops.
Performance: (At 46,500 lb/21 092 kg) Cruising speed, 268 mph (231 km/h) at 15,000 ft (4 570 m); typical search speed, 161 mph (259 km/h) at 2,000 ft (610 m); range (max. fuel and 20% reserve), 2,661 mls (4 282 km), (with 10,000-lb/ 4 536-kg payload), 1,164 mls (1 873 km); time on station (at 230 mls/370 km from base with 20% reserve), 8·9 hrs; service ceiling, 25,000 ft (7 620 m).
Weights: Typical empty operational, 27,556 lb (12 500 kg); max. take-off, 46,500 lb (21 092 kg).
Accommodation: Basic crew of five comprising two pilots, a tactical navigator and two observer/despatchers. A routine navigator may be accommodated if required.
Status: Prototype conversion of company-owned BAe 748 demonstrator flown on February 18, 1977. Basic BAe 748 Series 2B being built at rate of one monthly at beginning of 1979.
Notes: The Coastguarder is a derivative of the BAe 748 Series 2A short- to medium-range transport (see 1976 edition) with tip-to-tip integral wing fuel tankage, ventral MEL Marec search radar and a sophisticated tactical navigation system. The extended wingtips of the Coastguarder are being applied to the BAe 748 Series 2B transport, which, with Dart 536-2 engines, was scheduled to fly early 1979 and replaces the Series 2A in production. A total of 335 BAe 748s in all versions had been sold by the beginning of 1979.

BAe COASTGUARDER

Dimensions: Span, 102 ft 6 in (31,23 m); length, 67 ft 0 in (20,42 m); height, 24 ft 10 in (7,57 m).

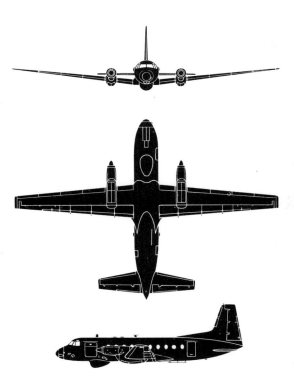

BAe HS 125–700

Country of Origin: United Kingdom.

Type: Light business executive transport.

Power Plant: Two 3,700 lb (1 680 kg) Garrett AiResearch TFE 731-3-1H turbofans.

Performance: High-speed cruise, 495 mph (796 km/h); long-range cruise, 449 mph (722 km/h); range (with 1,200-lb/544-kg payload and 45 min reserve), 2,705 mls (4 355 km); time to 35,000 ft (10 675 m), 19 min; operating altitude, 41,000 ft (12 500 m).

Weights: Typical basic, 13,327 lb (6 045 kg); max. take-off, 24,200 lb (10 977 kg).

Accommodation: Normal flight crew of two and basic lay-out for eight passengers, with alternative layouts for up to 14 passengers.

Status: Series 700 development aircraft flown June 28, 1976, followed by first production aircraft on November 8, 1976. Some 45 HS 125-700s had been delivered by the beginning of 1979, when production rate was three per month and firm orders had been placed for some 60 aircraft.

Notes: The HS 125-700 differs from the -600 (see 1976 edition) that it has supplanted primarily in having turbofans in place of Viper 601 turbojets. Various aerodynamic improvements have also been introduced. Two maritime surveillance versions of the HS 125-700 are on offer, these being the Protector I which retains accommodation for six passengers to provide dual-role capability, and the Protector II which is a dedicated single-role aircraft. Both versions will carry MEL Marec search radar. A successor to the HS 125–700, the HS 125-800 with supercritical wing, lengthened fuselage and, possibly, RB.401 engines, is under consideration.

BAe HS 125-700

Dimensions: Span, 47 ft 0 in (14,32 m); length, 50 ft 8½ in (15,46 m); height, 17 ft 7 in (5,37 m); wing area, 353 sq ft (32,80 m²).

BAe HARRIER G.R. MK. 3

Country of Origin: United Kingdom.
Type: Single-seat V/STOL strike and reconnaissance fighter.
Power Plant: One 21,500 lb (9 760 kg) Rolls-Royce Pegasus 103 vectored-thrust turbofan.
Performance: Max. speed, 720 mph (1 160 km/h) or Mach 0·95 at 1,000 ft (305 m), with typical external ordnance load, 640–660 mph (1 030–1 060 km) or Mach 0·85–0·87 at 1,000 ft (305 m); cruise, 560 mph (900 km/h) or Mach 0·8 at 20,000 ft (6 096 m); tactical radius for hi-lo-hi mission, 260 mls (418 km), with two 100 Imp gal (455 l) external tanks, 400 mls (644 km).
Weights: Empty, 12,400 lb (5 624 kg); max. take-off (VTO), 18,000 lb (8 165 kg); max. take-off (STO), 23,000+ lb (10 433+ kg); approx. max. take-off, 26,000 lb (11 793 kg).
Armament: Provision for two 30-mm Aden cannon with 130 rpg and up to 5,000 lb (2 268 kg) of ordnance.
Status: First of six pre-production aircraft flown August 31, 1966, with first of 77 G.R. Mk. 1s for RAF following December 28, 1967. Production of G.R. Mk. 1s and 13 T. Mk. 2s (see 1969 edition) for RAF completed. Production of 102 Mk. 50s (equivalent to G.R. Mk. 3) and eight Mk. 54 two-seaters (equivalent to T. Mk. 4) for US Marine Corps, and six Mk. 50s and two Mk. 54s ordered (via the USA) by Spain (by which known as Matador), plus follow-on orders for 13 G.R. Mk. 3s and four T Mk. 4s also completed. Production continuing in 1979 with follow-on orders for 24 Mk. 3s for the RAF, one Mk. 4 for the Royal Navy and five Mk. 50s for Spain.
Notes: RAF Harriers have been progressively brought up to G.R. Mk. 3 and T. Mk. 4 standards by installation of Pegasus 103 similar to that installed in Mk. 50 (AV-8A) for USMC.

BAE HARRIER G.R. MK. 3

Dimensions: Span, 25 ft 3 in (7,70 m); length, 45 ft 7$\frac{3}{4}$ in (13,91 m); height, 11 ft 3 in (3,43 m); wing area, 201·1 sq ft (18,68 m²).

BAe HAWK T. MK. 1

Country of Origin: United Kingdom.

Type: Two-seat multi-purpose trainer and light tactical aircraft.

Power Plant: One 5,340 lb (2 422 kg) Rolls-Royce Turboméca RT.172-06-11 Adour 151 turbofan.

Performance: Max. speed, 622 mph (1 000 km/h) at sea level or Mach 0·815, 580 mph (933 km/h) at 36,000 ft (10 970 m) or Mach 0·88; radius of action (HI-LO-HI profile with 5,600-lb/2 540-kg weapons load), 345 mls (560 km), (with 3,000-lb/1 360-kg weapons load and two 100 Imp gal/455 l drop tanks), 645 mls (1 040 km); time to 30,000 ft (9 145 m), 6·1 min; service ceiling, 48,000 ft (14 630 m).

Weights: Empty, 8,040 lb (3 647 kg); loaded (clean), 11,100 lb (5 040 kg); max. take-off, 17,085 lb (7 757 kg).

Armament: (Weapon training) one fuselage centreline and two wing stores stations each stressed for 1,120 lb (508 kg), and (attack) two additional similarly-stressed wing stations. Max. external stores load of 5,600 lb (2 540 kg).

Status: Single pre-production example flown August 21, 1974, first production example flown May 19, 1975, and some 80 delivered by beginning of 1979 against RAF orders for 175 aircraft. Fifty ordered by Finland, eight by Indonesia and 12 by Kenya. Forty-six of those ordered by Finland are to be assembled by Valmet from sets of components supplied by parent company. Production rate of five per month at beginning of 1979.

Notes: Development of combat version being actively pursued at beginning of 1979, when version with 5,700 lb (2 585 kg) Adour RT.172-56 to be tested and single-seat version under consideration.

BAe HAWK T. MK. 1

Dimensions: Span, 30 ft 9⅜ in (9,39 m); length, 38 ft 10⅔ in (11,85 m); height, 13 ft 1 in (4,00 m); wing area, 179·64 sq ft (16,69 m²).

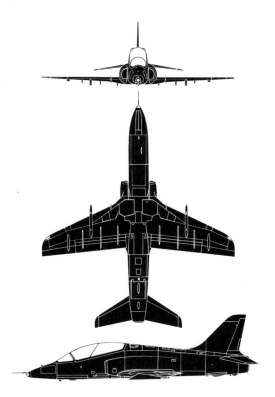

BAe NIMROD

Country of Origin: United Kingdom.

Type: Long-range maritime patrol aircraft.

Power Plant: Four 12,160 lb (5 515 kg) Rolls-Royce RB. 168-20 Spey Mk. 250 turbofans.

Performance: Max. speed, 575 mph (926 km/h); max. transit speed, 547 mph (880 km/h); econ. transit speed, 490 mph (787 km/h); typical ferry range, 5,180–5,755 mls (8 340–9 265 km); typical endurance, 12 hrs.

Weights: Max. take-off, 177,500 lb (80 510 kg); max. overload (eight new-build Mk. 1s), 192,000 lb (87 090 kg).

Armament: Ventral weapons bay accommodating full range of ASW weapons (homing torpedoes, mines, depth charges, etc) plus two underwing pylons on each side for total of four Aérospatiale AS.12 ASMs (or AS.11 training rounds).

Accommodation: Normal operating crew of 12 with two pilots and flight engineer on flight deck and nine navigators and sensor operators in tactical compartment.

Status: First of two Nimrod prototypes employing modified Comet 4C airframes flown May 23, 1967. First of initial batch of 38 production Nimrod M.R. Mk. 1s flown on June 28, 1968. Completion of this batch in August 1972 followed by delivery of three Nimrod R. Mk. 1s for special electronics reconnaissance, and eight more M.R. Mk. 1s ordered in 1973. Eleven M.R. Mk. 1s to be rebuilt as A.E.W. Mk. 3s of which fully representative prototype to fly 1980, and remainder being progressively brought up to M.R. Mk. 2 standard with first to be delivered late 1979.

Notes: M.R. Mk. 2 is result of refit programme, changes including new EMI radar, new sonics system, improved navigational and display systems, and increased computer capacity.

BAe NIMROD

Dimensions: Span, 114 ft 10 in (35,00 m); length, 126 ft 9 in (38,63 m); height, 29 ft 8½ in (9,01 m); wing area, 2,121 sq ft (197,05 m²).

BAe SEA HARRIER F.R.S. MK. 1

Country of Origin: United Kingdom.
Type: Single-seat V/STOL shipboard multi-role fighter.
Power Plant: One 21,500 lb (9 760 kg) Rolls-Royce Pegasus 104 vectored-thrust turbofan.
Performance: (Estimated) Max. speed, 720 mph (1 160 km/h) at 1,000 ft (305 m) or Mach 0·95, with two Martel ASMs and two Sidewinder AAMs, 640–660 mph (1 030–1 060 km/h) or Mach 0·85–0·87; tactical radius (intercept mission with two 100 Imp gal/455 l drop tanks, two 30-mm cannon and two Sidewinder AAMs), 450 mls (725 km), (strike mission HI-LO-HI profile), 330 mls (480 km).
Weights: Empty, 12,500 lb (5 670 kg); max. STO take-off, 22,500 lb (10 206 kg); max. overload, 25,000 lb (11 339 kg).
Armament: Provision for two (flush-fitting) podded 30-mm Aden cannon with 130 rpg beneath fuselage. Five external hardpoints (one fuselage and four wing) each stressed for 1,000 lb (453,5 kg), with max. external ordnance load for STO (excluding cannon) of 5,000 lb (2 268 kg). Typical loads include two Martel or Harpoon ASMs on inboard wing pylons and two Sidewinder AAMs on outboard pylons.
Status: First Sea Harrier (built on production tooling) flown on August 21, 1978, with three development and evaluation aircraft to fly first half of 1979. Deliveries of 34 for Royal Navy from late 1979.
Notes: Intended for use for the Royal Navy from three *Invincible*-class command cruisers, all of which will be equipped with "ski-jump" launching ramps, the Sea Harrier should be compared with the McDonnell Douglas AV-8B (see pages 148–149). The Indian Navy announced its intention in October 1978 of procuring the Sea Harrier from about 1980 onwards.

BAE SEA HARRIER F.R.S. MK. 1

Dimensions: Span, 25 ft 3 in (7,70 m); length, 47 ft 7 in (14,50 m); height, 12 ft 2 in (3,70 m); wing area, 201·1 sq ft (18,68 m²).

BAE-AÉROSPATIALE CONCORDE

Countries of Origin: United Kingdom and France.
Type: Long-range supersonic commercial transport.
Power Plant: Four 38,050 lb (17 259 kg) reheat Rolls-Royce/SNECMA Olympus 593 Mk. 602 turbojets.
Performance: Max. cruise, 1,354 mph (2 179 km/h) at 51,300 ft (15 635 m) or Mach 2·05; range with max. fuel (22,250-lb/10 092-kg payload and FAR reserves), 3,915 mls (6 300 km), with max. payload (28,000 lb/12 700 kg) at Mach 0·93 at 30,000 ft (9 145 m), 3,063 mls (4 930 km), at Mach 2·05, 3,869 mls (6 226 km); initial climb rate, 5,000 ft/min (25,4 m/sec); service ceiling (approx.), 60,000 ft (18 300 m).
Weights: Operational empty, 174,750 lb (79 265 kg); max. take-off, 400,000 lb (181 435 kg).
Accommodation: Normal flight crew of three and one-class seating for 128 passengers. Alternative high-density arrangement for 144 passengers.
Status: First and second prototypes flown March 2 and April 9, 1969, respectively. First of two pre-production aircraft flew December 17, 1971, and the first production example following on December 6, 1973, 13 further aircraft having flown by the beginning of 1979, two remaining to be completed during the course of the year.
Notes: The Concorde began to operate its first fare-paying passenger services in January 1976, these being initiated simultaneously by British Airways and Air France which have five and four Concordes respectively. Joint operation of a Concorde service between London and Singapore was initiated by British Airways and Singapore Airlines in December 1977, and suspended after one week, but this service was to be resumed early 1979. Conditional purchase agreements with Iran Air (three) and the Civil Aviation Administration of China (three) had not been taken up by the beginning of 1979, when five Concordes remained unsold.

38

BAE-AÉROSPATIALE CONCORDE

Dimensions: Span, 83 ft 10 in (25,56 m); length, 202 ft 3⅜ in (61,66 m); height, 37 ft 1 in (11,30 m); wing area, 3,856 sq ft (358,25 m²).

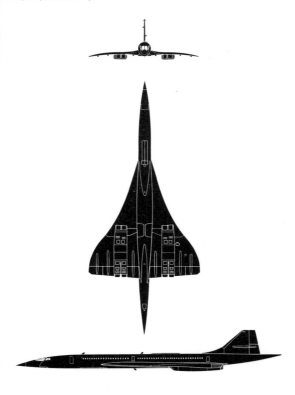

BEECHCRAFT DUCHESS 76

Country of Origin: USA.

Type: Light cabin monoplane.

Power Plant: Two 180 hp Avco Lycoming O-360-A1G6D six-cylinder horizontally-opposed engines.

Performance: Max. speed, 197 mph (317 km/h); max. cruise (at 3,600 lb/1 634 kg), 191 mph (307 km/h) at 6,000 ft (1 830 m); normal cruise, 176 mph (283 km/h) at 10,000 ft (3 050 m); econ. cruise, 172 mph (277 km/h) at 12,000 ft (3 658 m); range at econ. cruise (45 min reserves), 898 mls (1 445 km); initial climb, 1,248 ft/min (6,3 m/sec).

Weights: Empty, 2,446 lb (1 110 kg); max. take-off, 3,900 lb (1 770 kg).

Accommodation: Pilot and three passengers in individual seats, with provision for up to 180 lb (81,6 kg) of baggage in separate compartment.

Status: Prototype flown September 1974, production being initiated in the spring of 1977, and the first production example flying on May 24, 1977. First deliveries were made early 1978, and some 140 had been delivered by the beginning of 1979, with 200 plus scheduled for delivery during that year.

Notes: Bearing a close resemblance to the Piper PA-44 Seminole (see pages 176–177), the Duchess embodies handed propellers and honeycomb-bonded wings. It is being marketed through Beech Aero Centers at which it is now becoming the primary twin trainer.

BEECHCRAFT DUCHESS 76

Dimensions: Span, 38 ft 0 in (11,58 m); length, 29 ft 0 in (8,84 m); height, 9 ft 6 in (2,89 m); wing area, 181 sq ft (16,81 m²).

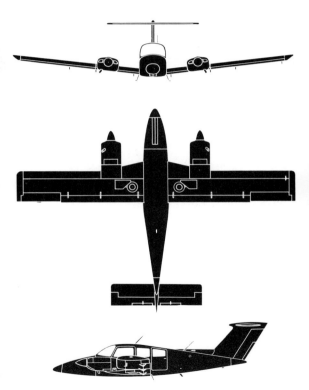

BEECHCRAFT SKIPPER 77

Country of Origin: USA.
Type: Side-by-side two-seat primary trainer.
Power Plant: One 115 hp Avco Lycoming O-235 four-cylinder horizontally-opposed engine.
Performance: No details available at time of closing for press, but maximum speed reportedly in excess of 130 mph (209 km/h) at sea level, with max. continuous cruise (75% power) exceeding 120 mph (193 km/h) at 8,500 ft (2 590 m).
Weights: Max. take-off, 1,650 lb (748 kg).
Status: Prototype of the Skipper 77 flown (as the PD 285) on February 6, 1975, a decision to initiate production being taken during the course of 1976, and a production prototype flying early September 1978. Certification was expected in January 1979, with first production deliveries commencing shortly thereafter.
Notes: The Skipper 77 primary trainer has been evolved as a low-cost, high-volume-production aircraft, placing emphasis on simplicity of maintenance and low operating cost, and is directly competitive with the closely similar Piper PA-38 Tomahawk (see pages 172–173). Both models utilise wings incorporating NASA-developed high-lift aerofoil sections and a T-type tail configuration which is claimed to offer more positive rudder control and enhanced stability. It is intended to market the Skipper through Beech Aero Centers (of which there are nearly 100 with more than 5,000 members).

BEECHCRAFT SKIPPER 77

Dimensions: Span, 30 ft 0 in (9, 14 m); length, 23 ft 10¾ in (7,28 m); height, 7 ft 6½ in (2,30 m).

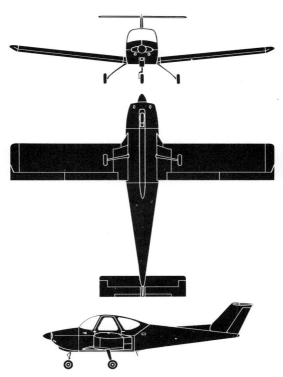

BEECHCRAFT T-34C (TURBINE MENTOR)

Country of Origin: USA.

Type: Tandem two-seat primary trainer.

Power Plant: One 680 shp (derated to 400 shp) Pratt & Whitney (Canada) PT6A-25 turboprop.

Performance: Max. cruise, 213 mph (343 km/h) at sea level, 239 mph (384 km/h) at 10,000 ft (3 050 m); range (5% and 20 min reserve), 787 mls (1 265 km) at 220 mph (354 km/h) at 17,500 ft (5 340 m), 915 mls (1 470 km) at 222 mph (357 km/h) at 25,000 ft (7 625 m); initial climb, 1,430 ft/min (7,27 m/sec).

Weights: Empty equipped, 3,015 lb (1 368 kg); normal loaded, 4,249 lb (1 927 kg).

Status: First of two YT-34Cs flown September 21, 1974, and production continuing at beginning of 1979 against total US Navy requirement for some 278 aircraft. Export T-34C-1 delivered to Morocco, Ecuador, Peru, Algeria and Indonesia during 1978.

Notes: Updated derivative of Continental 0-470-13-powered Model 45, the T-34C is fitted with a torque-limited PT6A-25 turboprop affording 400 shp, but the T-34C-1 may be fitted with a version of the PT6A-25 derated to 550 shp, wing racks for external ordnance and an armament control system to permit operation as an armament trainer or light counter-insurgency aircraft. With a max. take-off weight of 5,425 lb (2 460 kg), the T-34C-1 has two 600-lb (272-kg) capacity wing inboard stores stations and two 300-lb (136 kg) capacity outboard stations,

BEECHCRAFT T-34C (TURBINE MENTOR)

Dimensions: Span, 33 ft 4¾ in (10,18 m); length, 28 ft 8½ in (8,75 m); height, 9 ft 10⅞ in (3,02 m); wing area, 179·56 sq ft (16,66 m²).

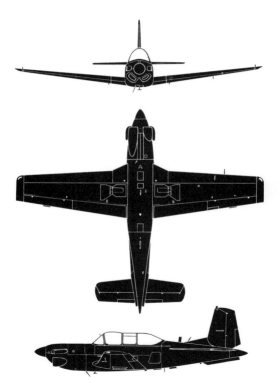

BOEING MODEL 727-200

Country of Origin: USA.

Type: Short- to medium-range commercial transport.

Power Plant: Three 14,500 lb (6 577 kg) Pratt & Whitney JT8D-9 turbofans (with 15,000 lb/6 804 kg JT8D-11s or 15,500 lb/7 030 kg JT8D-15s as options).

Performance: Max. speed, 621 mph (999 km/h) at 20,500 ft (6 250 m); max. cruise, 599 mph (964 km/h) at 24,700 ft (7 530 m); econ. cruise, 570 mph (917 km/h) at 30,000 ft (9 145 m); range with 26,400-lb (11 974-kg) payload and normal reserves, 2,850 mls (4 585 km), with max. payload (41,000 lb/18 597 kg), 1,845 mls (2 970 km).

Weights: Operational empty (basic), 97,525 lb (44 235 kg), (typical), 99,000 lb (44 905 kg); max. take-off, 208,000 lb (94 347 kg).

Accommodation: Crew of three on flight deck and six-abreast seating for 163 passengers in basic arrangement with max. seating for 189 passengers.

Status: First Model 727-100 flown February 9, 1963, with first delivery (to United) following October 29, 1963. Model 727-200 flown July 27, 1967, with first delivery (to North-east) on December 11, 1967. Deliveries from mid-1972 have been of the so-called "Advanced 727-200" (to which specification refers and illustrations apply) and sales of Model 727s had attained 1,618 at the beginning of 1979, with 1,427 delivered and production running at 11 aircraft monthly.

Notes: The Model 727-200 is a "stretched" version of the 727-100 (see 1972 edition). Deliveries of the "Advanced 727" with JT8D-17 engines of 16,000 lb (7 257 kg), permitting an increase of 3,500 lb (1 587 kg) in payload, began (to Mexicana) in June 1974. The 1,282nd Model 727 delivered in August 1977 was Boeing's 3,000th jetliner. Almost two-thirds of all Model 727 sales have been of -200 series aircraft.

BOEING MODEL 727-200

Dimensions: Span, 108 ft 0 in (32,92 m); length, 153 ft 2 in (46,69 m); height, 34 ft 0 in (10,36 m); wing area, 1,700 sq ft (157,9 m²).

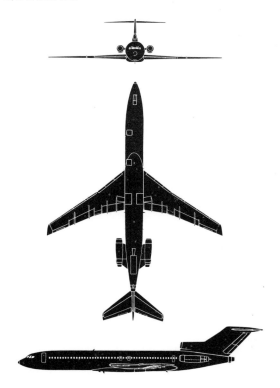

BOEING MODEL 737-200

Country of Origin: USA.

Type: Short-haul commercial transport.

Power Plant: Two 14,500 lb (6 577 kg) Pratt & Whitney JT8D-9 turbofans.

Performance: Max. speed, 586 mph (943 km/h) at 23,500 ft (7 165 m); max. cruise (at 90,000 lb/40 823 kg), 576 mph (927 km/h) at 22,600 ft (6 890 m); econ. cruise, 553 mph (890 km/h) at 30,000 ft (9 145 m); range (max. fuel and reserves), 2,530 mls (4 075 km), (max. payload of 34,790 lb/ 15 780 kg and reserves), 2,370 mls (3 815 km).

Weights: Operational empty, 60,210 lb (27 310 kg); max. take-off, 115,500 lb (52 390 kg).

Accommodation: Flight crew of two and up to 130 passengers in six-abreast seating with alternative arrangement for 115 passengers.

Status: Model 737 initially flown on April 9, 1967, with first deliveries (737-100 to Lufthansa) same year. Stretched 737-200 flown on August 8, 1967, with deliveries (to United) in 1968. Total sales were 683 (including 19-200s delivered to USAF as T-43A navigational trainers—see 1975 edition) by the beginning of 1979, with 548 delivered and production running at three monthly.

Notes: All aircraft delivered since May 1971 have been completed to the so-called "Advanced 737-200/C/QC" standard embodying improvements in range and short-field performance. JT8D-15 or -17 engines are optional and a max. take-off weight option of 117,000 lb (53 070 kg) is available, while a 128,600 lb (58 332 kg) take-off weight was expected to be certificated early in 1979, with a commensurate payload increase, this having called for strengthening in a number of areas.

BOEING MODEL 737-200

Dimensions: Span, 93 ft 0 in (28,35 m); length, 100 ft 0 in (30,48 m); height, 37 ft 0 in (11,28 m); wing area, 980 sq ft (91,05 m²).

BOEING MODEL 747-200B

Country of Origin: USA.

Type: Long-range large-capacity commercial transport.

Power Plant: Four 47,000 lb (21 320 kg) Pratt & Whitney JT9D-7W turbofans.

Performance: Max. speed at 600,000 lb (272 155 kg), 608 mph (978 km/h) at 30,000 ft (9 150 m); long-range cruise, 589 mph (948 km/h) at 35,000 ft (10 670 m); range with max. fuel and FAR reserves, 7,080 mls (11 395 km), with 79,618-lb (36 114-kg) payload, 6,620 mls (10 650 km); cruise ceiling, 45,000 ft (13 715 m).

Weights: Operational empty, 361,216 lb (163 844 kg); max. take-off, 775,000 lb (351 540 kg).

Accommodation: Normal flight crew of three and basic accommodation for 66 first-class and 308 economy-class passengers. Alternative layouts for 447 or 490 economy-class passengers nine- and 10-abreast respectively.

Status: First Model 747-100 flown on February 9, 1969, and first commercial services (by Pan American) inaugurated January 22, 1970. The first Model 747-200 (747B), the 88th aircraft off the assembly line, flown October 11, 1970. Orders (excluding SP) had passed 410 by the beginning of 1979, when production was rising to seven monthly.

Notes: Principal versions are the -100 and -200 series, the latter having greater fuel capacity and increased maximum take-off weight, convertible passenger/cargo and all-cargo versions of the -200 series being designated 747-200C and 747-200F. The first production example of the latter flew on November 30, 1971. Deliveries of the Model 747SR, a short-range version of the 747-100 (to Japan Air Lines), began September 1973. The 747-200B was flown on June 26, 1973 with 51,000 lb (23 133 kg) General Electric CF6-50D engines, and the 52,500 lb (23 810 kg) CF6-50E and the 52,000 lb (23 585 kg) Rolls-Royce RB.211-524 are offered as options.

BOEING MODEL 747-200B

Dimensions: Span, 195 ft 8 in (59,64 m); length, 231 ft 4 in (70,51 m); height, 63 ft 5 in (19,33 m); wing area, 5,685 sq ft (528,15 m²).

BOEING MODEL 747SP

Country of Origin: USA.

Type: Long-haul commercial transport.

Power Plant: Four 46,950 lb (21 296 kg) Pratt & Whitney JT9D-7A turbofans.

Performance: Max. cruise, 594 mph (957 km/h) at 35,000 ft (10 670 m); econ. cruise, 570 mph (918 km/h) at 35,000 ft (10 670 m); long-range cruise, 555 mph (893 km/h); range (with max. payload of 97,080 lb/44 034 kg), 6,620 mls (10 650 km), (with max. fuel and 30,000-lb/13 608-kg payload), 9,570 mls (15 400 km).

Weights: Operational empty, 315,000 lb (140 878 kg); max. take-off, 660,000 lb (299 370 kg).

Accommodation: Flight crew of three and basic accommodation for 28 first-class and 288 economy-class passengers. Max. high-density arrangement for 360 passengers in 10-abreast seating.

Status: First production Model 747SP flown July 4, 1975, with first customer deliveries (to Pan Am) following early 1976. Thirty-two ordered by beginning of 1979.

Notes: The SP (Special Performance) version of the Model 747 embodies a reduction in overall length of 47 ft 7 in (14,30 m) and retains a 90% commonality of components with the standard Model 747 (see pages 50–51). The Model 747SP is intended primarily for operation over long-range routes where traffic densities are insufficient to support the standard model. Apart from having a shorter fuselage, the Model 747SP has taller vertical tail surfaces with a double-hinged rudder and new trailing-edge flaps. CAAC became 60th Boeing 747 customer on December 16, 1978, with an order for three (and option on two more) 747SPs.

BOEING MODEL 747SP

Dimensions: Span, 195 ft 8 in (59,64 m); length, 184 ft 9 in (56,31 m); height, 65 ft 5 in (19,94 m); wing area, 5,685 sq ft (528,15 m²).

BOEING E-3A SENTRY

Country of Origin: USA.

Type: Airborne warning and control system aircraft.

Power Plant: Four 21,000 lb (9 525 kg) Pratt & Whitney TF33-PW-100/100A turbofans.

Performance: No details have been released for publication, but max. and econ. cruise speeds are likely to be generally similar to those of the equivalent commercial Model 707-320B (i.e., 627 mph/1 010 km/h and 550 mph/886 km/h respectively). Mission requirement is for 7-hr search at 29,000 ft (8 840 m) at 1,150 mls (1 850 km) from base. Unrefuelled endurance, 11·5 hrs.

Weights: Empty equipped, 170,000 lb (77 110 kg); max. take-off, 325,000 lb (147 418 kg).

Accommodation: Operational crew of 17 comprising flight crew of four, systems maintenance team of four, a battle commander and an air defence operations team of eight.

Status: First of two (EC-137D) development aircraft flown February 9, 1972, one being converted to pre-production standard. Two pre-production aircraft following in 1975, with first 14 production aircraft delivered to the USAF's 52nd Airborne Warning and Control Wing by beginning of 1979, when 25 Sentries had been funded with procurement of three per year planned through 1983 to provide total of 31 aircraft. Seven Sentries are on order for 1979–80 delivery to Iran.

Notes: The procurement of 18 E-3A Sentries for operation by NATO (excluding the UK) was being finalised at the beginning of 1979, when planning called for initial delivery to NATO in 1982 and final full deployment following in 1984. Production No 24 Sentry is expected to be the first for NATO operation. The Sentry was scheduled to assume a role in US continental air defence from the beginning of 1979.

BOEING E-3A SENTRY

Dimensions: Span, 145 ft 9 in (44,42 m); length, 152 ft 11 in (46,61 m); height, 42 ft 5 in (12,93 m); wing area, 3,050 sq ft (283,4 m²).

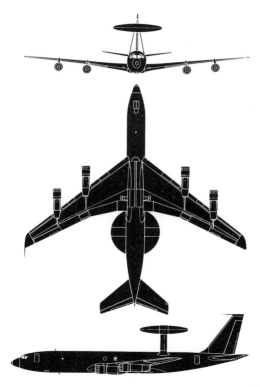

BRITTEN-NORMAN BN2B ISLANDER

Country of Origin: United Kingdom.
Type: Light utility transport.
Power Plant: Two (BN2B-26/27) 260 hp Avco Lycoming 0-540-E4C5 or (BN2B-20/21) 300 hp IO-540-K1B5 six-cylinder horizontally-opposed engines.
Performance: (BN2B-20) Max. speed, 180 mph (290 km/h) at sea level; cruise (75% power), 164 mph (264 km/h) at 700 ft (215 m), (67% power), 158 mph (254 km/h) at 9,000 ft (2 745 m), (59% power), 152 mph (244 km/h) at 12,000 ft (3 660 m); range (75% power), 639 mls (1 028 km), (at 59% power), 706 mls (1 136 km); initial climb, 1,130 ft/min (5,74 m/sec); service ceiling, 18,000 ft (5 485 m).
Weights: Empty weight (standard equipment), 4,043 lb (1 834 kg); max. take-off, 6,600 lb (2 994 kg).
Accommodation: Flight crew of one or two and up to nine passengers (one beside pilot and four double seats).
Status: Prototype Islander flown on June 12, 1965, and first production aircraft on August 20, 1966. Approximately 900 had been ordered by beginning of 1979 (the 800th having been delivered on November 14, 1978) when combined production in UK and Romania was running at 8–10 monthly. The BN2B prototype was first flown late August 1978, and this sub-type replaced the BN2A in production from 1979.
Notes: BN2B is current production standard Islander with two different engines and optional wingtip auxiliary fuel tank extensions (BN2B-21 and -27). The Defender and Maritime Defender (see 1978 edition) are military and coastal surveillance versions.

BRITTEN-NORMAN BN2B ISLANDER

Dimensions: Span, 49 ft 0 in (14,94 m); length, 35 ft 7¾ in (10,86 m); height, 13 ft 8¾ in (4,18 m); wing area, 325 sq ft (30,19 m²).

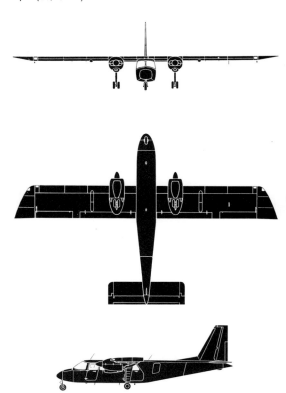

CANADAIR CL-600 CHALLENGER

Country of Origin: Canada.
Type: Light business executive transport.
Power Plant: Two 7,500 lb (3 405 kg) Avco Lycoming ALF 502L turbofans.
Performance: Max. speed, 581 mph (935 km/h) at 36,000 ft (10 975 m) or Mach 0·88; high-speed cruise, 575 mph (925 km/h) or Mach 0·86; range cruise, 528 mph (850 km/h) or Mach 0·8; optimum cruise, 502 mph (807 km/h) or Mach 0·76; range (with 3,000-lb/1 362-kg payload), 980 mls (1 577 km) at Mach 0·85, 3,392 mls (5 458 km) at Mach 0·83, 4,030 mls (6 485 km) at Mach 0·8; time to 41,000 ft (12 495 m), 17 min.
Weights: Empty, 13,567 lb (6 160 kg); basic operational, 17,100 lb (7 763 kg); max. take-off, 32,500 lb (14 742 kg).
Accommodation: Basic flight crew of two and executive layouts for 8–14 passengers.
Status: First Challenger (built on production jigs) flown on November 8, 1978, and more than 100 announced orders by beginning of 1979, with first (No 6 airframe) scheduled to be handed over to a customer in August–September. Production rate of up to seven per month expected to be attained in 1980.
Notes: A "stretched" Challenger with 15 ft (4,57 m) longer fuselage and a weight of approx. 43,000 lb (19 522 kg) is projected, this being able to accommodate 50 passengers in four-abreast seating.

CANADAIR CL-600 CHALLENGER

Dimensions: Span, 61 ft 10 in (18,85 m); length, 68 ft 5 in (20,85 m); height, 20 ft 8 in (6,30 m); wing area, 450 sq ft (41,81 m²).

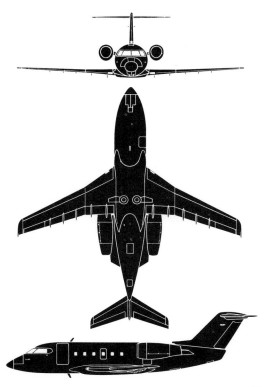

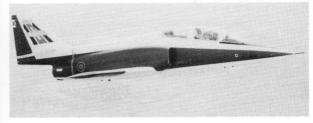

CASA C-101 AVIOJET

Country of Origin: Spain.
Type: Two-seat basic and advanced trainer.
Power Plant: One 3,500 lb (1 588 kg) Garrett AiResearch TFE 731-2-2J turbofan.
Performance: (At 10,362 lb/4 700 kg) Max. speed, 479 mph (770 km/h) or Mach 0·7 at 28,000 ft (8 535 m), 404 mph (650 km/h) or Mach 0·53 at sea level; time to 25,000 ft (7 620 m), 12 min; service ceiling, 41,000 ft (12 495 m); range (internal fuel at 11,540 lb/5 235 kg), 2,485 mls (4 000 km); max. climb (at 10,362 lb/4 700 kg), 3,350 ft/min (17 m/sec).
Weights: Basic operational empty, 6,790 lb (3 080 kg); loaded (pilot training mission with outer wing tanks empty), 10,362 lb (4 700 kg), (with max. internal fuel), 11,540 lb (5 235 kg); max. take-off, 12,346 lb (5 600 kg).
Armament: Seven external stores stations (six wing and one fuselage) for maximum of 3,307 lb (1 500 kg) of ordnance. Provision is made for a semi-recessed pod beneath the aft cockpit for a 30-mm cannon or two 7,62-mm Miniguns. Warload options include four Mk. 83 or six Mk. 82 bombs, or four AGM-65 Maverick missiles.
Status: Four prototypes of which first flown on June 29, 1977, and last on April 17, 1978. Sixty ordered by Spanish Air Force in March 1978, of which first scheduled to be delivered October 1979 with last being delivered March 1981.
Notes: The Aviojet is scheduled to achieve operational status by early 1980, the Northrop Corporation having been responsible for the air intake design and wing section, and Messerschmitt-Bölkow-Blohm having designed the rear fuselage and tail.

CASA C-101 AVIOJET

Dimensions: Span, 34 ft 9$\frac{3}{8}$ in (10,60 m); length, 40 ft 2$\frac{1}{4}$ in (12,25 m); height, 13 ft 11 in (4,25 m); wing area, 215·3 sq ft (20,00 m²).

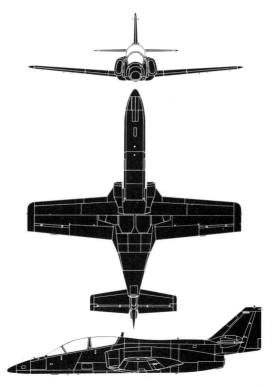

CASA C-212-200 AVIOCAR

Country of Origin: Spain.
Type: STOL utility transport.
Power Plant: Two 850 shp Garrett AiResearch TPE 331-10-501C turboprops.
Performance: (At 16,094 lb/7 300 kg) Max. cruising speed, 242 mph (390 km/h) at 10,000 ft (3 050 m); initial climb, 1,730 ft/min (8,79 m/sec); range (high-speed cruise, max. fuel, 1,070 mls (1 720 km), (max. payload—4,960 lb/2 250 kg), 472 mls (760 km).
Weights: Max. take-off, 16,094 lb (7 300 kg).
Accommodation: Flight crew of two and 18 passengers in three-abreast seating in commercial configuration, 12 casualty stretchers in aeromedical configuration, or up to 20 troops or up to 4,960 lb (2 250 kg) of freight in military configuration.
Status: Prototype of C-212-200 (the 138th production Aviocar) flown in April 1978, with production deliveries scheduled for third quarter of 1979.
Notes: The C-212-200 differs from the initial production version of the Aviocar (see 1977 edition), now known as the C-212-100, in having uprated engines, some structural strengthening of the main frames and centre wing skin, a stronger undercarriage and increased tailplane area. The C-212-200, which complements the -100 in production, offers improved payload/range characteristics. Some 150 -100 Aviocars had been manufactured by the beginning of 1979, sales having been made in 10 countries. An assembly line has been established in Indonesia (where 82 are to be completed by 1982), and deliveries to the Spanish Air Force have included navigational training and photographic versions.

CASA C-212-200 AVIOCAR

Dimensions: Span, 62 ft 4 in (19,00 m); length, 49 ft 10½ in (15,20 m); height, 20 ft 8¾ in (6,32 m); wing area, 430·56 sq ft (40,00 m²).

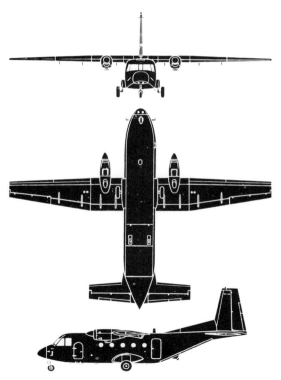

CESSNA 402C

Country of Origin: USA.

Type: Light business and utility transport.

Power Plant: Two 325 hp Teledyne Continental TSIO-520-VB six-cylinder horizontally-opposed engines.

Performances: Max. speed, 266 mph (428 km/h) at 16,000 ft (4 875 m); max. cruise (72% power), 223 mph (359 km/h) at 10,000 ft (3 050 m), 245 mph (395 km/h) at 20,000 ft (6 095 m); max. range (with 45 min reserve), 1,420 mls (2 286 km) at 168 mph (270 km/h) at 10,000 ft (3 050 m); initial climb, 1,450 ft/min (7,36 m/sec); service ceiling, 26,900 ft (8 200 m).

Weights: Empty (standard utility), 4,105 lb (1 862 kg); max. take-off, 6,850 lb (3 107 kg).

Accommodation: Two seats side-by-side with dual control in pilot's compartment and four individual seats plus two double seats in main cabin of Utililiner version, or four individual seats plus two optional seats in Businessliner version.

Status: The Model 402C replaced the Model 402 in the Cessna line from October 1978.

Notes: The 1979 Model 402C differs from the original Model 402 (see 1970 edition), in continuous production since 1969, in having a higher aspect ratio "wet" wing of bonded construction, new undercarriage and uprated engines.

CESSNA 402C

Dimensions: Span, 44 ft 1½ in (13,44 m); length, 36 ft 4½ in (11,09 m); height, 11 ft 5⅝ in (3,49 m); wing area, 225·8 sq ft (20,98 m²).

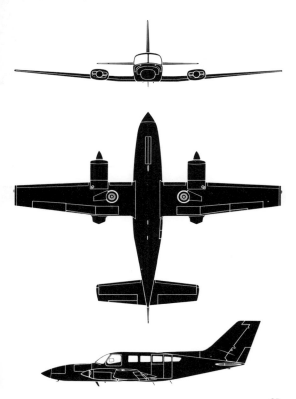

CESSNA 414A CHANCELLOR

Country of Origin: USA.

Type: Light executive and utility transport.

Power Plant: Two 310 hp Teledyne Continental TSIO-520-NB six-cylinder horizontally-opposed engines.

Performance: Max. speed, 275 mph (443 km/h) at 20,000 ft (6 095 m); max. cruise (74·8% power), 222 mph (358 km/h) at 10,000 ft (3 050 m), 258 mph (415 km/h) at 24,500 ft (7 470 m); max. range, 1,490 mls (2 340 km) at 166 mph (267 km/h) at 10,000 ft (3 050 m); initial climb, 1,580 ft/min (8 m/sec); service ceiling, 31,350 ft (9 555 m).

Weights: Standard empty, 4,354 lb (1 975 kg); max. take-off, 6,750 lb (3 062 kg).

Accommodation: Two seats side-by-side in pilot's compartment and various optional arrangements for up to six passengers in main cabin.

Status: The Model 414 Chancellor was first introduced in December 1969, an extensively revised model (described here) being offered for 1978, during which year production averaged 12 monthly and was continuing at that rate at the beginning of 1979.

Notes: The current production model of the Chancellor, the 414A, differs from the Model 414 that it supplants in having a longer-span "wet" wing of bonded construction which results in the elimination of the wingtip tanks previously standard, a longer fuselage and a new hydraulically-operated undercarriage. The cabin pressure differential has also been increased.

CESSNA 414A CHANCELLOR

Dimensions: Span, 44 ft $1\frac{1}{2}$ in (13,44 m); length, 36 ft $4\frac{1}{2}$ in (11,09 m); height, 11 ft $5\frac{5}{8}$ in (3,49 m); wing area, 225·8 sq ft (20,98 m²).

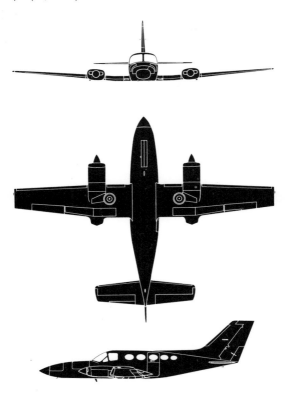

CESSNA 441 CONQUEST

Country of Origin: USA.

Type: Light business executive transport.

Power Plant: Two 625 shp Garrett AiResearch TPE331-8-401S turboprops.

Performance: Max. speed, 338 mph (545 km/h) at 16,000 ft (4 875 m); max. cruise, 332 mph (534 km/h) at 18,000 ft (5 485 m); range cruise, 283 mph (456 km/h); range (with eight passengers and 45 min reserve), 1,595 mls (2 566 km) at max. cruise at 33,000 ft (10 060 m), 1,632 mls (2 626 km) at range cruise at 33,000 ft (10 060 m); initial climb, 2,435 ft/min (12,36 m/sec); service ceiling, 37,000 ft (11 280 m).

Weights: Empty equipped, 5,487 lb (2 489 kg); max. take-off, 9,850 lb (4 468 kg).

Accommodation: Two seats side-by-side on flight deck and maximum of nine passengers in main cabin.

Status: Prototype flown on August 26, 1975, with first customer delivery on September 24, 1977. Approximately 80 delivered by beginning of 1979, when production was averaging 10 aircraft per month.

Notes: Cessna's first turboprop-driven business aircraft, the Conquest slots between the company's piston-engined twins and the turbofan-powered Citation series.

CESSNA 441 CONQUEST

Dimensions: Span, 49 ft 4 in (15,04 m); length, 39 ft $0\frac{1}{4}$ in (11,89 m); height, 13 ft $1\frac{3}{4}$ in (4,01 m); wing area, 253·6 sq ft (23,56 m²).

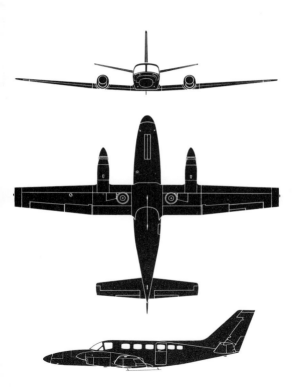

CESSNA CITATION II

Country of Origin: USA.
Type: Light business executive transport.
Power Plant: Two 2,500 lb (1 135 kg) Pratt & Whitney (Canada) JT15D-4 turbofans.
Performance: Max. cruise, 420 mph (676 km/h) at 25,400 ft (7 740 m); range cruise, 380 mph (611 km/h) at 43,000 ft (13 105 m); range (with eight passengers and 45 min reserve), 2,080 mls (3 347 km) at 380 mph (611 km/h); initial climb, 3,500 ft/min (17,8 m/sec); time to 41,000 ft (12 495 m), 34 min; max. cruise altitude, 43,000 ft (13 105 m).
Weights: Typical empty equipped, 6,960 lb (3 160 kg); max. take-off, 12,500 lb (5 675 kg).
Accommodation: Normal flight crew of two on separate flight deck and up to 10 passengers in main cabin.
Status: Two prototypes of Citation II flown January 31 and April 28, 1977, respectively, with first customer deliveries commencing late March 1978, with some 40 delivered by the beginning of 1979 when production rate was increasing from six to eight aircraft monthly (plus six Citation Is). The 500th Citation was delivered in the late autumn of 1978.
Notes: The Citation II is a stretched (4 ft/1,22 m longer cabin) version of the original Citation, with a higher aspect ratio wing, uprated engines and increased fuel capacity, and is being manufactured in parallel with the Citation I and I/SP (the latter catering for single-pilot operation) with similar accommodation to the first Citation, JT15D-1A turbofans and a 47 ft 1 in/14,36 m wing. Citation I deliveries began in February 1977. The Citation III (see pages 72–73), which is being added to Cessna's range of turbofan-powered light business executive transports for 1980 delivery, is not expected to affect the production tempo of the Citation I and II.

CESSNA CITATION II

Dimensions: Span, 51 ft 8 in (15,76m); length, 47 ft 3 in (14,41 m); height, 14 ft 11 in (4,55 m).

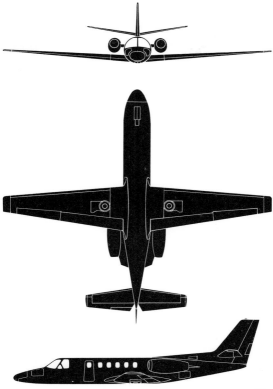

CESSNA CITATION III

Country of Origin: USA.

Type: Light business executive transport.

Power Plant: Two 3,700 lb (1 680 kg) Garrett AiResearch TFE 731-3-100S turbofans.

Performance: (Estimated) Cruising speed (at 13,700 lb/ 6 214 kg), 540 mph (869 km/h) at 33,000 ft (10 060 m); range (basic aircraft) with four passengers, 2,875 mls (4 626 km), with 10 passengers, 2,190 mls (3 524 km); (extended-range version) with four passengers, 3,450 mls (5 550 km), with 10 passengers, 2,750 mls (4 425 km); climb (at 17,000 lb/7711 kg), 11 min to 35,000 ft (10 665 m), 18 min to 41,000 ft (12 500 m).

Weights: Empty, 9,325 lb (4 230 kg), (extended-range), 9,400 lb (4 264 kg); max. take-off, 17,000 lb (7 711 kg), (extended-range), 18,300 lb (8 301 kg).

Accommodation: Normal flight crew of two on separate flight deck and up to 10 passengers in main cabin. Standard interior has four forward-facing and four aft-facing individual seats.

Status: The Citation III is scheduled to fly in May 1979, with a second prototype in October 1979. First production aircraft is expected to be completed in January 1981, with 25 to be built during year and first customer deliveries in May.

Notes: Despite its name, the Citation III has no commonality with the Citation II (see pages 70–71). The Citation III is offered in basic and extended-range versions, the latter augmenting the integral wing tanks with a fuselage tank.

CESSNA CITATION III

Dimensions: Span, 53 ft 4 in (16,30 m); length, 55 ft 2½ in (16,80 m); height, 17 ft 0 in (5,20 m); wing area, 312 sq ft (29,00 m²).

DASSAULT-BREGUET FALCON 10

Country of Origin: France.
Type: Light business executive transport.
Power Plant: Two 3,230 lb (1465 kg) Garrett-AiResearch TFE 731-2 turbofans.
Performance: Max. cruising speed, 567 mph (912 km/h) at 30,000 ft (9145 m), 495 mph (796 km/h) or Mach 0·75 at 45,000 ft (13 715 m); range (four passengers and 45 min reserve), 2070 mls (3 330 km) at 45,000 ft (13 715 m), 1,495 mls (2 070 km) at max. cruise at 30,000 ft (9 145 m).
Weights: Empty equipped, 10,760 lb (4 880 kg); max. take-off, 18,740 lb (8 500 kg).
Accommodation: Flight crew of two and various arrangements for four–seven passengers in main cabin.
Status: First of three prototypes flown December 1, 1970, followed by first production aircraft on April 30, 1973. Approximately 150 ordered by beginning of 1979, with 130 delivered and production running at 2·5 monthly.
Notes: Essentially a scaled-down Falcon 20, the Falcon 10 (alias Mystère 10) can be equipped for liaison, nav-attack and systems training, aerial photography and aeromedical tasks, and navigational aid calibration, and two have been delivered to France's *Aéronavale* (Mystère 10MER) for communications tasks and the radar training of Super Etendard pilots. The *Aéronavale* has an option on three additional aircraft of this type.

DASSAULT-BREGUET FALCON 10

Dimensions: Span, 42 ft 11 in (13,08 m); length, 45 ft 5¾ in (13,86 m); height, 15 ft 1 in (4,61 m); wing area, 259·4 sq ft (24,1 m²).

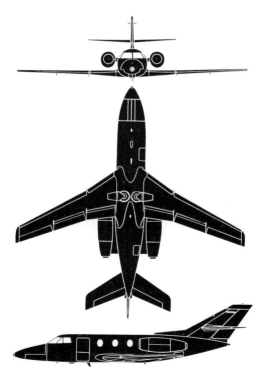

DASSAULT-BREGUET HU-25A GUARDIAN (FALCON 20G)

Country of Origin: France.

Type: Medium-range maritime surveillance aircraft.

Power Plant: Two 5,300 lb (2 404 kg) Garrett AiResearch ATF3-6-2C turbofans.

Performance: Max. speed, 540 mph (869 km/h) at 41,000 ft (12 495 m); patrol speed, 240 mph (386 km/h) at 2,000 ft (610 m); range (max. payload and reduced fuel with 45 min reserve), 1,840 mls (2 960 km) at 40,000 ft (12 190 m); max. range (five crew, full avionics and 45 min reserve), 2,500 mls (4 020 km).

Weights: Empty equipped, 18,705 lb (8 485 kg); max. take-off, 32,000 lb (14 515 kg).

Accommodation: Two pilots with full dual control, a surveillance systems operator and two observers. Provision for radar operator's seat and couch for three passengers.

Status: Prototype of Falcon 20G was flown on November 28, 1977, with first delivery of HU-25A version to US Coast Guard planned for December 1979 against order for 41 aircraft to be delivered subsequently at rate of one per month. Orders for all versions of the Falcon 20 totalled some 440 aircraft by the beginning of 1979, with approximately 400 delivered.

Notes: Derived from the Falcon 20F (see 1974 edition) to meet a US Coast Guard requirement for a medium-range maritime surveillance aircraft to replace the Grumman Albatross amphibian, the HU-25A Guardian (alias Falcon 20G) is intended to fulfil search-and-rescue and marine environmental protection missions, secondary tasks including the surveillance of territorial waters, logistics support, short-range aids to navigation and marine science activities. Existing Falcons can be retrofitted with ATF3-6 turbofans and some 50 retrofits had been ordered by the beginning of 1979.

DASSAULT-BREGUET HU-25A GUARDIAN (FALCON 20G)

Dimensions: Span, 53 ft 5¾ in (16,30 m); length, 56 ft 2⅞ in (17,14 m); height, 17 ft 0¾ in (5,20 m); wing area, 449·93 sq ft (41,80 m²).

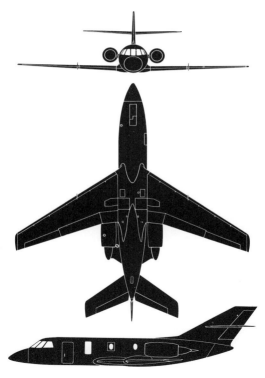

DASSAULT-BREGUET FALCON 50

Country of Origin: France.

Type: Light business executive transport.

Power Plant: Three 3,700 lb (1 680 kg) Garrett AiResearch TFE 731-3 turbofans.

Performance: Max. cruise, 560 mph (900 km/h) at 30,000 ft (9 145 m), or Mach 0·83; long-range cruise, 495 mph (792 km/h) at 37,000 ft (11 275 m), or Mach 0·75; range (with eight passengers and 45 min plus 173-mile/288-km reserve), 3,800 mls (6 115 km) at long-range cruise, 3,454 mls (5 560 km) at 528 mph (850 km/h), or Mach 0·8; max. operating altitude, 41,000 ft (12 500 m).

Weights: Empty equipped, 19,840 lb (9 000 kg); max. take-off, 37,480 lb (17 000 kg).

Accommodation: Flight crew of two and various cabin arrangements for six to ten passengers.

Status: First prototype flown November 7, 1976, with second flown on February 16, 1978, and the first pre-series aircraft following on June 13, 1978. First production delivery is scheduled for March 1979, and production rate will be one per month until October 1979, increasing to three—four monthly thereafter. Orders totalled some 80 aircraft by 1979.

Notes: Subsequent to initial flight testing, the first prototype Falcon 50 was modified to incorporate a supercritical wing which, having the same planform as the original wing, resulted in significant improvements in speed, range, climb and fuel consumption. The first prototype established two world records (straight line distance and speed) on October 9, 1977, while flying from New York to Paris, and in September 1978, the first pre-series aircraft established a further record by flying from Chicago to Paris in 8·5 hours.

DASSAULT-BREGUET FALCON 50

Dimensions: Span, 62 ft 2⅖ in (18,96 m); length, 60 ft 9 in (18,52 m); height, 22 ft 10⅖ in (6,97 m); wing area, 504·13 sq ft (46,83 m²).

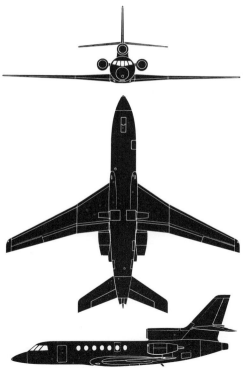

DASSAULT-BREGUET MIRAGE F1

Country of Origin: France.

Type: Single-seat multi-purpose fighter.

Power Plant: One 11,023 lb (5 000 kg) dry and 15,873 lb (7 200 kg) reheat SNECMA Atar 9K-50 turbojet.

Performance: Max. speed (clean), 915 mph (1 472 km/h) or Mach 1·2 at sea level, 1,450 mph (2 335 km/h) or Mach 2·2 at 39,370 ft (12 000 m); range cruise, 550 mph (885 km/h) at 29,530 ft (9 000 m); range with max. external fuel, 2,050 mls (3 300 km), with max. external combat load of 8,818 lb (4 000 kg), 560 mls (900 km), with external combat load of 4,410 lb (2 000 kg), 1,430 mls (2 300 km); service ceiling, 65,600 ft (20 000 m).

Weights: Empty, 16,314 lb (7 400 kg); loaded (clean), 24,030 lb (10 900 kg); max. take-off, 32,850 lb (14 900 kg).

Armament: Two 30-mm DEFA cannon and (intercept) 1-3 Matra 530 Magic and two AIM-9 Sidewinder AAMs.

Status: First of four prototypes flown December 23, 1966. First production for *Armée de l'Air* flown February 15, 1973. Production rate of five per month at beginning of 1979. Licence manufacture is being undertaken in South Africa. Firm orders totalled more than 550 aircraft by beginning of 1979, including Greece, 40 (F1CG), Kuwait, 20 (18 F1CK and two F1BK), Libya, 38 (32 F1ED and six F1BD), Iraq, 36 (inc. four F1B), Morocco, 50 (F1CH), South Africa, 48 (16 F1CZ and 32 F1AZ), Spain, 63 (F1CE), and Ecuador, 18. The *Armée de l'Air* orders totalled 179 aircraft by the beginning of 1979 against planned total procurement of 225 of which 105 delivered by end of 1978

Notes: Production versions currently comprise F1A and F1E for ground attack role, the former for VFR operations only, the F1BD tandem two-seat conversion trainer, nine of which were ordered by the *Armée de l'Air* in 1978, and the F1C interceptor.

DASSAULT-BREGUET MIRAGE F1

Dimensions: Span, 27 ft 6¾ in (8,40 m); length, 49 ft 2½ in (15,00 m); height, 14 ft 9 in (4,50 m); wing area, 269·098 sq ft (25 m²).

DASSAULT-BREGUET MIRAGE 2000

Country of Origin: France.
Type: Single-seat multi-role fighter.
Power Plant: One 19,840 lb (9 000 kg) reheat SNECMA M53-5 turbofan (bypass turbojet).
Performance: Max. attainable speed, 1 550 mph (2 495 km/h) above 36,090 ft (11 000 m) or Mach 2·35; max. sustained speed, 1,452 mph (2 336 km/h) or Mach 2·0; time to Mach 2·0 at 49,200 ft (15 000 m) from brakes release (with four AAMs), 4 min; max. climb rate, 49,000 ft/min (249 m/sec); operational ceiling, 65,000 ft (19 810 m); tactical radius (four AAMs and two 374 Imp gal/1 700 l drop tanks), 435 mls (700 km).
Weights: Combat, 19,840 lb (9 000 kg); max. take-off, 33,070 lb (15 000 kg).
Armament: Two 30-mm DEFA 554 cannon and (air superiority) two Matra 550 Magic and two Matra Super 530 AAMs, or (strike) up to 11,000 lb (5 000 kg) of ordnance on nine external stations (four beneath wings and five beneath fuselage).
Status: First and second prototypes flown March 10 and September 18, 1978, respectively, with third prototype scheduled to fly early 1979. Fourth (two-seat' and fifth prototypes to fly early 1980, with first production aircraft at end of 1981, orders including four in the Fiscal 1979 budget, with 23 to be ordered in 1980, 43 in 1981 and 44 in 1982.
Notes: *Armée de l'Air* has a requirement for total of 200 Mirage 2000s for the air defence role with probable follow-on of similar quantity configured for interdiction and reconnaissance.

DASSAULT-BREGUET MIRAGE 2000

Dimensions: (Approximate) Span, 29 ft 6 in (9,00 m); length, 49 ft 2½ in (15,00 m); wing area, 450 sq ft (41,8 m²).

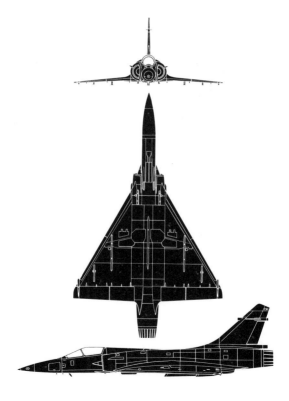

DASSAULT-BREGUET SUPER ÉTENDARD

Country of Origin: France.

Type: Single-seat shipboard strike fighter.

Power Plant: One 11,025 lb (5 000 kg) SNECMA Atar 8K-50 turbojet.

Performance: Max. speed, 745 mph (1 200 km/h) at 985 ft (300 m) or Mach 0·97, 695 mph (1 118 km/h) at 36,000 ft (11 000 m) or Mach 1·05; radius of action (hi-lo-hi with 2,200-lb/998-kg bomb load), 225 mls (360 km), (lo-lo-lo), 160 mls (260 km), (anti-shipping mission with AM-39 Exocet ASM and 1,700-lb/771-kg bomb load), 255 mls (410 km); initial climb, 19,685 ft/min (100 m/sec).

Weights: Empty, 14,220 lb (6 450 kg); max. take-off (catapult), 25,350 lb (11 500 kg); overload, 26,455 lb (12 000 kg).

Armament: Two 30-mm DEFA 552A cannon with 122 rpg and a variety of ordnance on five external stores stations (four wing and one fuselage), including Matra 550 Magic AAMs, AM-39 Exocet ASM, etc.

Status: First of three Super Étendard development aircraft (converted from Étendard airframes) flown on October 28, 1974, the second and third flying on March 28 and March 9, 1975, respectively. First production aircraft built against initial contracts for 50 flown November 24, 1977. Further 21 ordered in FY 1978 and FY 1979 to meet total requirement for 71. Production rate of two per month at beginning of 1979.

Notes: The Super Étendard is a more powerful derivative of the Etendard IVM (see 1965 edition) with new avionics, a revised wing and other changes. The Super Étendard is intended to serve aboard the carriers *Clémenceau* and *Foch,* and the first aircraft was delivered to the French Navy on June 28, 1978, and nine had been accepted by 1979.

84

DASSAULT-BREGUET SUPER ÉTENDARD

Dimensions: Span, 31 ft 6 in (9,60 m); length, 46 ft 11½ in (14,31 m); height, 12 ft 8 in (3,85 m); wing area, 306·77 sq ft (28,50 m²).

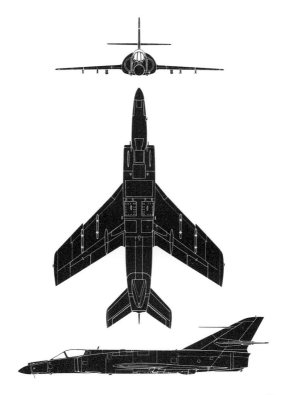

DASSAULT-BREGUET SUPER MIRAGE 4000

Country of Origin: France.
Type: Single-seat long-range strike fighter.
Power Plant: Two 19,840 lb (9 000 kg) reheat SNECMA M53-5 turbofans (bypass turbojets).
Performance: (Estimated) Max. sustained speed, 1,452 mph (2 336 km/h) or Mach 2·2 above 36,090 ft (11 000 m), 915 mph (1 472 km/h) or Mach 1·2 at sea level; max. climb rate, 50,000 ft/min (254 m/sec); operational ceiling, 65,000 ft (19 810 m).
Weights: (Estimated) Loaded (clean), 37,500 lb (17 000 kg).
Armament: Two 30-mm DEFA 554 cannon and up to 15,000 lb (6 804 kg) of ordnance on nine external stations (four wing and five fuselage).
Status: Prototype Super Mirage 4000 was scheduled to commence its flight test programme in February 1969.
Notes: Optimised for the deep penetration role, the Super Mirage 4000 has been developed as a private venture, the *Armée de l'Air* currently possessing no requirement for an aircraft in this category, and closely resembles the Mirage 2000 (see pages 82–83) in aerodynamic, structural and systems layout, but is an appreciably larger aircraft. The Super Mirage 4000 is most closely comparable with the McDonnell Douglas F-15 Eagle and, like the Mirage 2000, its features include fly-by-wire, artificial stability, leading-edge flaps and carbon-fibre composites.

DASSAULT-BREGUET SUPER MIRAGE 4000

Dimensions: No details available for publication.

DASSAULT-BREGUET/DORNIER ALPHA JET

Countries of Origin: France and Federal Germany.

Type: Two-seat basic-advanced trainer and light tactical aircraft.

Power Plant: Two 2,975 lb (1 350 kg) SNECMA-Turboméca Larzac 04-C5 turbofans.

Performance: Max. speed, 622 mph (1 000 km/h) at sea level or Mach 0·816, 567 mph (912 km/h) at 32,810 ft (10 000 m) or Mach 0·84; tactical radius (training mission LO-LO-LO profile), 267 mls (430 km); ferry range (max. internal fuel), 1,243 mls (2 000 km), (with two 68 Imp gal/310 l external tanks), 1,678 mls (2 700 km); max. climb, 11,220 ft/min (57 m/sec); ceiling, 45,000 ft (13 715 m).

Weights: Empty, 7,716 lb (3 500 kg); normal loaded (clean), 11,023 lb (5 000 kg); normal take-off (close air support), 13,448 lb (6 100 kg); max. overload, 15,983 lb (7 250 kg).

Armament: External centreline gun pod with (Alpha Jet E) 30-mm DEFA 533 or (Alpha Jet A) 27-mm Mauser cannon. Two 1,500-lb (680-kg) and two 750-lb (340-kg) capacity wing stores stations with max. load of 4,850 lb (2 200 kg).

Status: First of four prototypes flown October 26, 1973, with first production Alpha Jet E flying on November 4, 1977, and first production Alpha Jet A on April 12, 1978. Production rate of 13 per month in France and six per month in Germany scheduled for late 1979. Orders at beginning of 1979 called for 144 for France, 175 for Germany, 33 for Belgium, 24 for Morocco, 12 for Ivory Coast and five for Togo, and agreement for licence manufacture in Egypt (approx. 160 aircraft) signed on September 17, 1978.

Notes: Two final assembly lines (Toulouse and Munich) respectively building Alpha Jet E trainer for *Armée de l'Air* and Alpha Jet A close air support aircraft for *Luftwaffe*.

DASSAULT-BREGUET/DORNIER ALPHA JET

Dimensions: Span, 29 ft 11 in (9,11 m); length, 40 ft 3 in (12,29 m); height, 13 ft 9 in (4,19 m); wing area, 188 sq ft (15,50 m²).

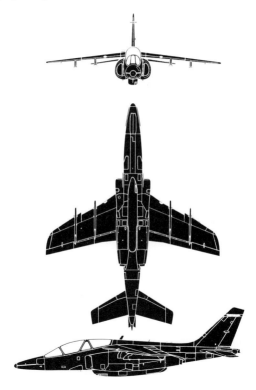

DE HAVILLAND CANADA DASH 7

County of Origin: Canada.

Type: STOL short-haul commercial transport.

Power-Plant: Four 1,120 shp Pratt & Whitney (Canada) PT6A-50 turboprops.

Performance: Max. cruise, 269 mph (434 km/h) at 15,000 ft (4 570 m); long-range cruise, 235 mph (379 km/h) at 20,000 ft (6 560 m); range (with 12,150-lb/5 511-kg payload), 696 mls (1 120 km); max. range, 1,807 mls (2 910 km).

Weights: Empty equipped, 26, 850 lb (12 179 kg); max. take-off, 43,500 lb (19 731 kg).

Accommodation: Flight crew of two and standard seating arrangement for 50 passengers in pairs on each side of central aisle with 300 cu ft (8,49 m³) baggage compartment or 240 cu ft (6,80 m³) compartment and buffet. Various optional passenger/cargo arrangements (e.g., 34 passengers and one pallet, 26 passengers and two pallets or 18 passengers and three pallets.

Status: Two pre-production aircraft flown on March 27 and June 26, 1975. Production commitment for 50 aircraft, of which first flown April 1977, and first customer delivery (second production aircraft to Rocky Mountain) October 1977. Six aircraft had been delivered by the beginning of 1979, when orders totalled 32 aircraft and production rate was 1–1·5 monthly, rising to two monthly during year.

Notes: Current orders include two Dash 7s for the Canadian Armed Forces for operation in Europe and two examples of a maritime surveillance version, the Dash 7R Ranger, for the Canadian Coast Guard. The Ranger will be delivered in 1980 and will offer extended payload and range performance, increased fuel capacity providing a 10-hour flight capability. Two Dash 7s delivered to Wardair (one of which is illustrated above) are fitted with freight doors and have convertible interiors.

DE HAVILLAND CANADA DASH 7

Dimensions: Span, 93 ft 0 in (28,35 m); length, 80 ft 7¾ in (24,58 m); height, 26 ft 2 in (7,98 m); wing area, 860 sq ft (79,90 m²).

DORNIER DO 28D-5 TURBOSKY

Country of Origin: Federal Germany.
Type: Light utility transport.
Power Plant: Two 400 shp (derated from 646 shp) Avco Lycoming LTP 101-600 turboprops.
Performance: Max. cruising speed, 208 mph (335 km/h) at 10,000 ft (3 050 m); max. range (with two 55 Imp gal/250 l underwing auxiliary tanks), 1,430 mls (2 300 km); service ceiling, 30,840 ft (9 400 m).
Weights: Empty (with underwing tanks fitted), 4,903 lb (2 224 kg); max. take-off, 8,851 lb (4 015 kg).
Accommodation: Provision for two pilots with dual controls and up to 10 passengers in main cabin in individual seats and aft-, forward- or side-facing four-seat benches, side-benches for 12 troops, or (aeromedical role) five casualty stretchers and three seated casualties/medical attendants.
Status: Prototype TurboSky (converted from second prototype piston-engined Do 28D) flown on April 9, 1978. Production decision pending completion of flight test programme and market survey.
Notes: The Do 28D-5 is a turboprop-powered equivalent of the Do 28D-2 Skyservant (two 380 hp Avco Lycoming IGSO-540-A1E six-cylinder horizontally-opposed engines) which is currently in production. The original Do 28D prototype flew on February 23, 1966, and has since been in continuous production with a total of 250 sold by the beginning of 1979. By comparison with the Skyservant, the TurboSky offers improved performance and economy.

DORNIER DO 28D-5 TURBOSKY

Dimensions: Span, 51 ft 1 in (15,55 m); length, 37 ft 5 in (11,41 m); height, 12 ft 9½ in (3,90 m); wing area, 312·2 sq ft (29,00 m²).

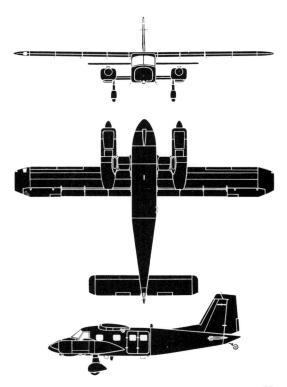

EMBRAER EMB-110P2 BANDEIRANTE

Country of Origin: Brazil.
Type: Third-level commuter transport.
Power Plant: Two 750 shp Pratt & Whitney (Canada) PT6A-34 turboprops.
Performance: Max. cruise (at 12,500 lb/5 670 kg), 262 mph (422 km/h) at 17,060 ft (5 200 m), (at 10,582 lb/4 800 kg), 267 mph (430 km/h) at 17,060 ft (5 200 m); range cruise, 224 mph (360 km/h); range (max. payload and 30 min reserve), 173 mls (278 km), (max. fuel and 1,307-lb/593-kg payload), 1,191 mls (1 916 km).
Weights: Empty equipped, 7,751 lb (3 416 kg); max. take-off, 12,500 lb (5 670 kg).
Accommodation: Two seats side-by-side on flight deck and 21 passengers in seven rows three abreast in main cabin.
Status: The first EMP-110P2 (146th Bandeirante) flown spring 1977 with production deliveries following during course of the year. Sales of the Bandeirante were expected to exceed 200 by the beginning of 1979 (including 80 for the Brazilian Air Force).
Notes: The Bandeirante has been the subject of continuous development since first prototype flew on October 26, 1968, and the EMB-110P2 is one of two stretched and more powerful versions introduced in 1977, the other being the EMB-110K1 military freighter featuring similar engines and fuselage stretch, a reinforced floor and upward-hinging cargo door. It can carry 3,868 lb (1 754 kg) of freight or 19 fully-equipped paratroops. Twenty EMB-110K1s have been delivered to the Brazilian Air Force, and further development of the basic EMB-110 design includes the EMB-120 30-seat commuter-liner, which, with a wider fuselage for three-abreast seating and 1,500 shp engines, is intended to complement the Bandeirante.

EMBRAER EMB-110P2 BANDEIRANTE

Dimensions: Span, 50 ft 3⅛ in (15,32 m); length, 49 ft 5¾ in (15,08 m); height, 15 ft 6¼ in (4,73 m); wing area, 312 sq ft (29,00 m²).

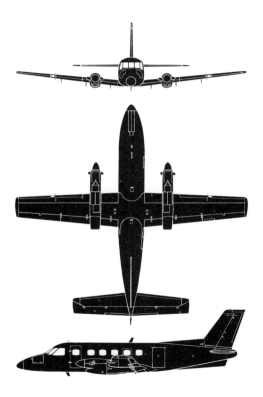

EMBRAER EMB-111M

Country of Origin: Brazil.

Type: Maritime patrol and coastal surveillance aircraft.

Power Plant: Two 750 shp Pratt & Whitney (Canada) PT6A-34 turboprops.

Performance: Max. cruise, 239 mph (385 km/h) at 9,840 ft (3 000 m); patrol speed, 198 mph (318 km/h) at 2,000 ft (610 m); endurance, 8–9 hrs; max. climb rate, 1,190 ft/min (6,04 m/sec); service ceiling, 23,700 ft (7 224 m).

Weights: Max. take-off, 15,432 lb (7 000 kg).

Accommodation: Basic crew of five comprising pilot, co-pilot, radar operator and two observers.

Armament: Provision may be made for six 5-in (12,7-cm) air-to-surface rockets to be carried, these being vertically disposed in pairs on three pylons (two beneath port wing and one beneath starboard).

Status: Sixteen EMB-111Ms ordered in 1976 for the Brazilian Air Force, including two prototypes, the first of which flew in July 1977. Six (EMB-111N) were ordered by the Chilean Navy and deliveries to both Brazilian and Chilean services were completed in 1978.

Notes: The EMB-111 is a derivative of the EMB-110 Bandeirante (see pages 94–95) with a wet wing, which, together with tip tanks, provides a total fuel capacity of 561 Imp gal (2 550 l), AN/APS-128 search radar mounted in a nose randome, provision for a 50-million candlepower searchlight mounted on the port wing, an LN-33 inertial navigation system, a chute for parachute flares and target markers, an eight-person inflatable lifeboat and other sea survival equipment. Application of the uprated -42 engine was under consideration at the beginning of 1979, this permitting a gross weight of 17,620 lb (8 000 kg).

EMBRAER EMB-111M

Dimensions: Span (over tip tanks), 52 ft 4¾ in (15,96 m); length, 48 ft 7⅞ in (14,83 m); height, 16 ft 6⅝ in (4,74 m); wing area, 312 sq ft (29,00 m²).

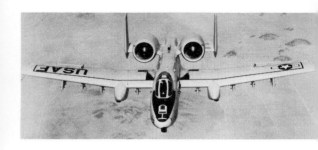

FAIRCHILD A-10A THUNDERBOLT II

Country of Origin: USA.

Type: Single-seat close-support aircraft.

Power Plant: Two 9,065 lb (4 112 kg) General Electric TF34-GE-100 turbofans.

Performance: (At 38,136 lb/17 299 kg) Max. speed, 433 mph (697 km/h) at sea level, 448 mph (721 km/h) at 10,000 ft (3 050 m); initial climb, 5,340 ft/min (27,12 m/sec); service ceiling, 34,700 ft (10 575 m); combat radius (with 9,540-lb/4 327-kg bomb load and 1,170 lb/531 kg of 30-mm ammunition, including 1·93 hr loiter at 5,000 ft/1 525 m), 288 mls (463 km) at (average) 329 mph (529 km/h) at 25,000–35,000 ft (7 620–10 670 m); ferry range, 2,487 mls (4 002 km).

Weights: Empty, 19,856 lb (9 006 kg); basic operational, 22,844 lb (10 362 kg); max. take-off, 46,786 lb (22 221 kg).

Armament: One seven-barrel 30-mm General Electric GAU-8 Avenger rotary cannon. Eleven external stations for maximum of 9,540 lb (4 327 kg) ordnance (with full internal fuel and 1,170 lb/531 kg 30-mm ammunition).

Status: First of two prototypes flown May 10, 1972, and first of six pre-production aircraft flown February 15, 1975. First production aircraft flown October 21, 1975, and some 160 of planned 733 Thunderbolt IIs to be procured (for USAF, Air National Guard and Air Force Reserve) delivered by beginning of 1979.

Notes: One of the six pre-production aircraft was scheduled to fly late spring 1979 after conversion as tandem two-seat night and adverse weather evaluation aircraft.

FAIRCHILD A-10A THUNDERBOLT II

Dimensions: Span, 57 ft 6 in (17,53 m); length, 53 ft 4 in (16,25 m); height, 14 ft 8 in (4,47 m); wing area, 506 sq ft (47,01 m²).

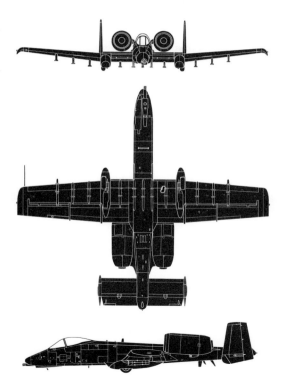

FOKKER F27MPA MARITIME

Country of Origin: Netherlands.
Type: Medium-range maritime patrol and surveillance aircraft.
Power Plant: Two 2,250 eshp Rolls-Royce Dart 536-7R turboprops.
Performance: Cruising speed (at 40,000 lb/18 145 kg), 265 mph (427 km/h) at 20,000 ft (6 095 m); typical search speed, 168 mph (270 km/h) at 2,000 ft (610 m); service ceiling (at 45,000 lb/20 412 kg), 23,000 ft (7 010 m); max. range (cruising at 20,000 ft/6 095 m with 30 min loiter and 5% reserves, with pylon tanks), 2,548 mls (4 100 km); max. endurance, 11 hrs.
Weights: Typical zero fuel, 28,097 lb (12 745 kg); max. take-off, 44,996 lb (20 410 kg).
Accommodation: Standard accommodation for crew of six comprising pilot, co-pilot, navigator, radar operator and two observers.
Status: Prototype F27 Maritime (converted F27 Mk 100 No. 68) flown on March 25, 1976, and first production aircraft was delivered in the summer of 1977. Initial customers were the Peruvian Navy (2) and the Spanish search and rescue service (3).
Notes: Derivative of Mk 400 transport with Litton AN/APS-503F search radar, Litton LTN-72 long-range inertial navigation system, blister windows adjacent to marine marker launcher and provision for pylon fuel tanks. The Maritime is ostensibly a civil patrol aircraft for off-shore "sovereignty" operations, such as oil-rig and fisheries protection, but has several potential military customers, being suitable for maritime reconnaissance. F27 orders (all versions) totalled 486 (excluding 205 built by Fairchild) at the beginning of 1979.

FOKKER F27MPA MARITIME

Dimensions: Span, 95 ft 1$\frac{4}{5}$ in (29,00 m); length, 77 ft 3$\frac{1}{2}$ in (23,56 m); height, 28 ft 6$\frac{7}{10}$ in; wing area, 753·47 sq ft (70.00 m²).

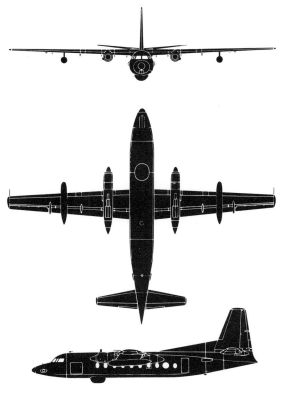

FOKKER F28 FELLOWSHIP MK. 4000

Country of Origin: Netherlands.

Type: Short-haul commercial transport.

Power Plant: Two 9,850 lb (4 468 kg) Rolls-Royce RB.183-2 Spey Mk 555-15H turbofans.

Performance: Max cruise, 523 mph (843 km/h) at 23,000 ft (7 000 m); econ. cruise, 487 mph (783 km/h) at 32,000 ft (9 755 m); range cruise, 421 mph (678 km/h) at 30,000 ft (9 145 m); range (with max. payload), 1,160 mls (1 870 km) at econ. cruise, (with max. fuel), 2,566 mls (4 130 km); max. cruise altitude, 35,000 ft (10 675 m).

Weights: Operational empty (typical), 37,736 lb (17 117 kg); max. take-off, 71,000 lb (32 200 kg).

Accommodation: Flight crew of two and typical single-class configuration for 85 passengers five abreast.

Status: First and second F28 prototypes flown May 9 and August 3, 1967, first delivery following on February 24, 1969. A total of 146 F28s (all versions) ordered by 1979.

Notes: The F28 Mks. 1000 and 2000 are now out of production (after completion of 97 and 10 respectively), having been replaced by the Mks. 3000 and 4000, both having unslatted, longer-span wings and Spey Mk. 555–15H engines. The former has the 80 ft 6½ in (24,55 m) fuselage of the Mk. 1000 and the latter has the longer fuselage of the Mk. 2000. Also on offer is the slatted Mk. 6000 (see 1977 edition) with the same high-density accommodation as the Mk. 4000 and having improved field performance and payload/range capabilities. A version proposed during 1978 is the Mk. 6600 which is a stretched version of the Mk. 6000 with 87 in (220 cm) inserted in the fuselage and Mk. 555-15K engines, and at the beginning of 1979, studies were continuing of the 115-seat-plus development of the F28, the F29.

102

FOKKER F28 FELLOWSHIP MK. 4000

Dimensions: Span, 82 ft 3 in (25,07 m); length 97 ft 1¾ in (29,61 m); height, 27 ft 9½ in (8,47 m); wing area, 850 sq ft (78,97 m²).

FOXJET ST600

Country of Origin: USA.
Type: Light business executive transport.
Power Plant: Two 850 lb (385 kg) Williams WR44-800 turbofans.
Performance: (Estimated) Max. speed, 410 mph (660 km/h) at 36,000 ft (10 975 m); cruise, 330 mph (531 km/h); range, 1,200 mls (1930 km) at 36,000 ft (10 975 m); initial climb, 3,400 ft/min (17,3 m/sec); service ceiling, 40,000 ft (12 200 m), time to 36,000 ft (10 970 m), 22 min.
Weights: Empty, 2,408 lb (1 092 kg); max. take-off, 4,449 lb (2 020 kg).
Accommodation: Pilot and five passengers in three side-by-side pairs.
Status: Prototype scheduled to fly in the summer of 1979, with customer deliveries commencing mid-1981.
Notes: The Foxjet ST600, which is being developed by Foxjet International, is the smallest turbofan-powered business executive transport yet designed, and will, it is claimed, be capable of operating from grass and other soft surfaces and offer a fuel cost less than that of a rented autombile. The wing of the Foxjet is of laminar section "which may be easily modified to a supercritical configuration" to cater for performance increases anticipated with the availability of more powerful versions of the Williams turbofan and is fitted with modified Fowler-type flaps to provide a high lift coefficient.

FOXJET ST600

Dimensions: Span, 31 ft 7 in (9,64 m); length, 31 ft 10 in (9,70 m); height, 10 ft 3 in (3,12 m); wing area, 125 sq ft (11,61 m²).

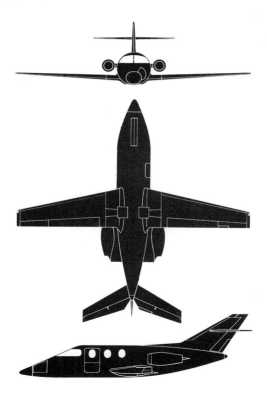

GAF NOMAD SEARCHMASTER

Country of Origin: Australia.
Type: Light maritime patrol and surveillance aircraft.
Power Plant: Two 400 shp Allison 250-B17B turboprops.
Performance: (Searchmaster B at 8,500 lb/3 855 kg) Max. cruising speed, 195 mph (313 km/h) at 5,000 ft (1 525 m); cruise (75% max. cruise rating), 176 mph (282 km/h); range (with 45 min reserve), 920 mls (1 482 km) at 10,000 ft (3 050 m); typical mission, 8 hr search at 161 mph (259 km/h) at 5,000 ft (1 525 m); initial climb, 1,460 ft/min (7,4 m/sec); service ceiling (at 8,000 lb/3 629 kg), 23,500 ft (7 165 m).
Weights: Operational empty (less equipment options), 4,783 lb (2 170 kg); max. take-off, 8,500 lb (3 855 kg).
Accommodation: Basic crew of four–five, comprising one or two pilots, a tactical navigator and one or two observer/despatchers.
Status: The Searchmaster is a derivative of the Nomad N22B light utility transport, the initial version, the Searchmaster B, being introduced in 1975, and the Searchmaster L commencing its test programme in 1978. Approximately 100 Nomads (all versions) had been completed by the beginning of 1979.
Notes: The Searchmaster B (described above) and Searchmaster L (illustrated) differ primarily in equipment fit, the former having a forward-looking Bendix RDR 1400 radar with 18-in (45,72-cm) scanner and the latter having Litton LASR 2 with a 36-in (91,44-cm) 360-deg scanner.

GAF NOMAD SEARCHMASTER

Dimensions: Span, 54 ft 0 in (16,46 m); length, 41 ft 2½ in (12,57 m); height, 18 ft 1½ in (5,52 m); wing area, 324 sq ft (30,10 m²).

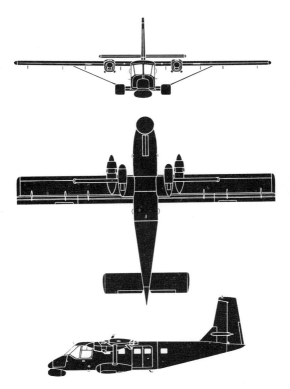

GATES LEARJET 28 LONGHORN

Country of Origin: USA.
Type: Light business executive transport.
Power Plant: Two 2,950 lb (1 340 kg) General Electric CJ610-8A turbojets.
Performance: Max. speed, 550 mph (885 km/h), or Mach 0·81; high-speed cruise, 501 mph (806 km/h) at 41,000–45,000 ft (12 495–13 715 m); econ. cruise, 460 mph (740 km/h) at 49,000–51,000 ft (14 935–15 545 m); max. range (with 1,200-lb/544-kg payload), 1,578 mls (2 540 km).
Weights: Empty equipped, 7,895 lb (3 581 kg); max. take-off, 15,000 lb (6 804 kg).
Accommodation: Two seats side-by-side on flight deck with dual controls and up to six passengers in cabin.
Status: Prototype of Learjet 28/29 flown on August 24, 1977, with first production model flown August 21, 1978, and first customer deliveries scheduled for early 1979 when production was running at nine (three Series 20 and six Series 30) monthly, with 900th Learjet scheduled for late spring delivery.
Notes: The Models 28 and 29 are basically improved versions of the Model 25, deliveries of which commenced in November 1967. The Models 28 and 29 differ in fuel capacity, that of the former being 580 Imp gal (2 637 l) and that of the latter being 654 Imp gal (2 973 l), and utilise the basic Model 25D wing with extended span and Whitcomb winglets of 6 sq ft (0,55 m²) area. The winglets improve cruise, landing characteristics and short-field performance. A further development combining the wing of the Learjet 28/29 with a longer and deeper fuselage offering "stand-up" cabin headroom is the Series 50 (Learjet 54/55/56 Longhorn). Accommodating 10 passengers, the Series 50 is to fly spring 1979, with customer deliveries mid-1980.

GATES LEARJET 28 LONGHORN

Dimensions: Span, 43 ft 9½ in (13,34 m); length, 47 ft 7⅗ in (14,52 m); height, 12 ft 3 in (3,73 m); wing area, 264·5 sq ft (24,57 m²).

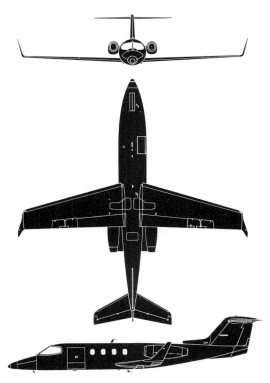

GENERAL DYNAMICS F-16

Country of Origin: USA.

Type: Single-seat air combat fighter (F-16A) and two-seat operational trainer (F-16B).

Power Plant: One (approx.) 25,000 lb (11 340 kg) reheat Pratt & Whitney F100-PW-100(3) turbofan.

Performance: Max. speed (with two Sidewinder AAMs), 1,255 mph (2 020 km/h) at 36,000 ft (10 970 m), or Mach 1·95, 915 mph (1 472 km/h) at sea level, or Mach 1·2; tactical radius (interdiction mission hi-lo-hi on internal fuel with six Mk. 82 bombs), 340 mls (550 km); ferry range, 2,300+ mls (3 700+ km); initial climb, 62,000 ft/min (315 m/sec); service ceiling, 52,000 ft (15 850 m).

Weights: Operational empty, 14,567 lb (6 613 kg); loaded (intercept mission with two Sidewinders), 22,785 lb (10 344 kg); max. take-off, 33,000 lb (14 969 kg).

Armament: One 20-mm M61A-1 Vulcan multi-barrel cannon with 515 rounds and max. external ordnance load of 15,200 lb (6 894 kg) with reduced internal fuel or 11,000 lb (4 990 kg) with full internal fuel distributed between nine stations (two wingtip, six underwing and one fuselage).

Status: First of two (YF-16) prototypes flown on January 20, 1974. First of eight pre-production aircraft (six single-seat F-16As and two two-seat F-16Bs) flown December 8, 1976, and first two-seater (fourth aircraft) on August 8, 1977, with the first full production F-16A flying on August 7, 1978. Current planning calls for 1,388 F-16s for USAF (including 204 F-16Bs), 160 (including 32 F-16Bs) for Iran and 75 for Israel. Licence manufacture by European consortium for Netherlands (84 plus 18 on option), Belgium (102 plus 14 on option), Denmark (48 plus 10 on option) and Norway (72).

GENERAL DYNAMICS F-16

Dimensions: Span (excluding missiles), 31 ft 0 in (9,45 m); length, 47 ft 7¾ in (14,52 m); height, 16 ft 5¼ in (5,01 m); wing area, 300 sq ft (27,87 m²).

GRUMMAN A-6E INTRUDER

Country of Origin: USA.

Type: Two-seat shipboard low-level strike aircraft.

Power Plant: Two 9,300 lb (4 218 kg) Pratt & Whitney J52-P-8A/B turbojets.

Performance: Max. speed (clean), 654 mph (1 052 km/h) at sea level or Mach 0·86, 625 mph (1 006 km/h) at 36,000 ft (10 970 m) or Mach 0·94, (close support role with 28 Mk. 81 Snakeye bombs), 557 mph (896 km/h) at 5,000 ft (1 525 m); combat range (clean), 2,320 mls (3 733 km) at 482 mph (776 km/h) average at 37,700—44,600 ft (11 500—13 600 m).

Weights: Empty, 25,980 lb (11 795 kg); max. take-off (field), 60,400 lb (27 420 kg), (catapult), 58,600 lb (26 605 kg).

Armament: Five external (one fuselage and four wing) stations each of 3,600 lb (1 635 kg) capacity for up to 15,000 lb (6 804 kg) of stores.

Status: Current production version of the Intruder, the A-6E, first flew on February 27, 1970, and as of September 1975, 66 new A-6Es had been built and 104 modified from A-6A standard. Programme called for last of 94 new-build A-6Es to be delivered in February 1976, but review of requirements led to request for 12 and 15 more in FY 1978 and FY 1979 respectively. Conversion of earlier models to A-6E standard (total of 228) extending through 1979.

Notes: All US Navy and US Marine Corps Intruders are being progressively updated to the latest A-6E standard with TRAM (Target Recognition Attack Multi-sensor) systems, FLIR (Forward-Looking Infra-Red) and CAINS (Carrier Airborne Inertial Navigation System), with fuselage air brakes deleted. The Intruder is also being modified to carry the Harpoon missile.

GRUMMAN A-6E INTRUDER

Dimensions: Span, 53 ft 0 in (16,15 m); length, 54 ft 9 in (16,69 m); height, 16 ft 2 in (4,93 m); wing area, 528·9 sq ft (49,14 m²).

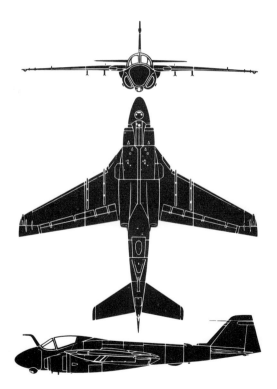

GRUMMAN E-2C HAWKEYE

Country of Origin: USA.

Type: Shipboard airborne early warning, surface surveillance and strike control aircraft.

Power Plant: Two 4,910 ehp Allison T56-A-425 turboprops.

Performance: Max. speed (at max. take-off), 348 mph (560 km/h) at 10,000 ft (3 050 m); max. range cruise, 309 mph (498 km/h); max. endurance, 6·1 hrs; mission endurance (at 230 mls/370 km from base), 4·0 hrs; ferry range, 1,604 mls (2 580 km); initial climb, 2,515 ft/min (12,8 m/sec); service ceiling, 30,800 ft (9 390 m).

Weights: Empty, 38,009 lb (17 240 kg); max. take-off, 51,900 lb (23 540 kg).

Accommodation: Crew of five comprising flight crew of two and Airborne Tactical Data System team of three, each at an independent operating station.

Status: First of two E-2C prototypes flown on January 20, 1971, with first production aircraft flying on September 23, 1972. Forty-six E-2Cs delivered by beginning of Fiscal Year 1979 against total US Navy requirement for 77 plus four for Israel (supplied during 1978).

Notes: Current production model of Hawkeye following 59 E-2As (all subsequently updated to E-2B standard) and, since December 1976, equipped with advanced APS-125 radar processing system.

GRUMMAN E-2C HAWKEYE

Dimensions: Span, 80 ft 7 in (24,56 m); length, 57 ft 7 in (17,55 m); height, 18 ft 4 in (5,59 m); wing area, 700 şq ft (65,03 m²).

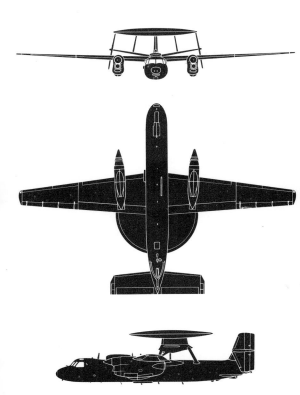

GRUMMAN F-14A TOMCAT

Country of Origin: USA.

Type: Two-seat shipboard multi-purpose fighter.

Power Plant: Two 20,900 lb (9 480 kg) reheat Pratt & Whitney TF30-P-412A turbofans.

Performance: Design max. speed (clean), 1,545 mph (2 486 km/h) at 40,000 ft (12 190 m) or Mach 2·34; max. speed (internal fuel and four AIM-7 missiles at 55,000 lb/24 948 kg), 910 mph (1 470 km/h) at sea level or Mach 1·2; tactical radius (internal fuel and four AIM-7 missiles plus allowance for 2 min combat at 10,000 ft/3 050 m), approx. 450 mls (725 km); time to 60,000 ft (18 290 m) at 55,000 lb (24 948 kg), 2·1 min.

Weights: Empty equipped, 40,070 lb (18 176 kg); normal take-off (internal fuel and four AIM-7 AAMs), 55,000 lb (24 948 kg); max. take-off (ground attack/interdiction), 68,567 lb (31 101 kg).

Armament: One 20-mm M-61A1 rotary cannon and (intercept mission) six AIM-7E/F Sparrow and four AIM-9G/H Sidewinder AAMs or six AIM-54A and two AIM-9G/H AAMs.

Status: First of 12 research and development aircraft flown December 21, 1970, and US Navy plans to acquire a total of 521 with more than 300 having been delivered by the beginning of 1979, but only 24 to be procured during course of current year. Delivery of 80 to Iranian Imperial Air Force completed August 1978. Iranian requirement for further 70 aircraft considered unlikely to be realised at beginning of 1979.

Notes: Although studies of possible higher-thrust engines for the Tomcat as a retrofit programme were continuing at the beginning of 1979, no replacement for the TF30 engines of the fighter has yet been funded.

GRUMMAN F-14A TOMCAT

Dimensions: Span (max.), 64 ft $1\frac{1}{2}$ in (19,55 m), (min.), 37 ft 7 in (11,45 m), (overswept on deck), 33 ft $3\frac{1}{2}$ in (10,15 m); length, 61 ft $11\frac{7}{8}$ in (18,90 m); height, 16 ft 0 in (4,88 m); wing area, 565 sq ft (52,5 m²).

GULFSTREAM AMERICAN GA-7 COUGAR

Country of Origin: USA.
Type: Light cabin monoplane.
Power Plant: Two 160 hp Avco Lycoming 0-320-D1D four-cylinder horizontally-opposed engines.
Performance: Max. speed, 193 mph (311 km/h) at sea level; max. cruise (75% power), 184 mph (296 km/h) at 8,500 ft (2 590 m); range cruise (45% power), 125 mph (202 km/h) at 8,500 ft (2 590 m); range at max. cruise, 967 mls (1 556 km) at 8,500 ft (2 590 m), at range cruise, 1,347 mls (2 167 km); initial climb, 1,160 ft/min (5,89 m/sec); service ceiling, 17,400 ft (5 305 m).
Weights: Empty, 2,588 lb (1 174 kg); max. take-off, 3,800 lb (1 724 kg).
Accommodation: Pilot and three passengers in individual seats. Baggage compartments in nose and rear fuselage with individual access doors.
Status: Prototype Cougar flown on December 20, 1974, with production prototype following on January 12, 1977. Production deliveries from February 1978, and some 70 Cougars had been delivered by the beginning of 1979, when production was 10—12 monthly, with 150—200 to be produced during year.
Notes: Developed by the former Grumman American Aviation Corporation (renamed Gulfstream American after acquisition by American Jet Industries), the Cougar makes extensive use of metal-to-metal bonding techniques and features integral wing fuel tanks. Projected derivatives include a turbo-supercharged model and a variant with 180 hp engines.

GULFSTREAM AMERICAN GA-7 COUGAR

Dimensions: Span, 36 ft 10½ in (11,23 m); length, 29 ft 10 in (9,10 m); height, 10 ft 4 in (3,16 m); wing area, 184 sq ft (17,10 m²).

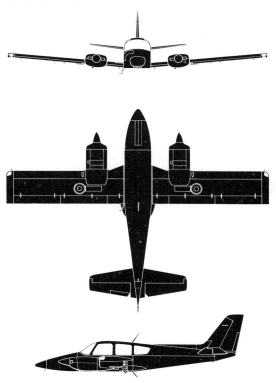

GULFSTREAM AMERICAN
GULFSTREAM III

Country of Origin: USA.

Type: Light business executive transport.

Power Plant: Two 11,400 lb (5176 kg) Rolls-Royce RB.163-25 Spey Mk. 511-8 turbofans.

Performance: (Estimated) Max. cruising speed, 560 mph (900 km/h) at 45,000 ft (13715 m) or Mach 0·85; long-range cruise, 511 mph (822 km/h) or Mach 0·775; max. range (with 1,600-lb/726-kg payload and 30 min reserve), 4,660 mls (7490 km).

Weights: Typical operational empty, 37,720 lb (17125 kg); max. take-off, 65,500 lb (29737 kg).

Accommodation: Crew of two or three and various layouts for up to 19 passengers in main cabin.

Status: Gulfstream III scheduled to fly on November 1, 1979, with first customer deliveries expected to commence mid-1980, and production of two monthly by August of that year.

Notes: The Gulfstream III is a progressive development of the (formerly Grumman) Gulfstream II (see 1969 edition) which has been in continuous production since 1965, and of which nearly 240 had been delivered by the beginning of 1979, with a total of 258 scheduled for completion before the earlier model is superseded by the Gulfstream III on the assembly line. The new variant has a lengthened fuselage by comparison with the Gulfstream II, a modified wing structure with NASA-style winglets, an extended nose radome, a wrap-around windscreen and improved crew accommodation. Gulfstream III wings are to be made available for retrofit to existing Gulfstream IIs from early 1981, the new wing affording improved range and field performance.

GULFSTREAM AMERICAN GULFSTREAM III

Dimensions: Span, 77 ft 10 in (23,72 m); length 82 ft 11 in (25,27 m); height, 23 ft 8 in (7,21 m); wing area, 934·6 sq ft (86,82 m²).

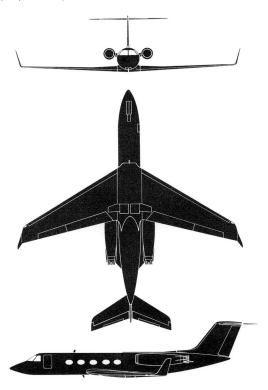

GULFSTREAM AMERICAN HUSTLER 500

Country of Origin: USA.

Type: Light business executive transport.

Power Plant: One 850 shp (derated from 1,089 shp) Pratt & Whitney PT6A-41 turboprop and one 2,200 lb (998 kg) Pratt & Whitney JT15D-1 turbofan.

Performance: (Estimated) Max. cruising speed, 460 mph (740 km/h) at 23,000 ft (7 010 m); econ. cruise, 403 mph (648 km/h) at 40,000 ft (12 190 m); range at max. cruise (45 min reserve), 1,290 mls (2 076 km), at econ. cruise, 2,296 mls (3 694 km); initial climb, 4,950 ft/min (25,1 m/sec); operating ceiling, 40,000 ft (12 190 m).

Weights: Empty, 4,681 lb (2 125 kg); max. take-off, 9,500 lb (4 313 kg).

Accommodation: Pilot and co-pilot/passenger on flight deck and five passengers in main cabin.

Status: The first prototype, known as the Hustler 400 and powered by the PT6A-41 turboprop only, was first flown on January 11, 1978, and was subsequently modified to aerodynamically represent more closely the twin-engined Hustler 500, the first of two pre-series examples of which is expected to be completed April 1979. Customer deliveries of the Hustler 500 are scheduled for early 1980.

Notes: Of centreline-thrust concept, Hustler 500 (turboprop in nose and turbofan in tail) is a progressive development of the Hustler 400 (see 1978 edition and photograph above) with a J115D-1 turbofan (replacing the small Williams WR19-3-1 turbofan proposed for the Hustler 400A), a lengthened fuselage with relocated cabin door, permanent wingtip fuel tanks and conventional ailerons in place of spoilers. Changes attributable to the testing of the Hustler 400 include a lower tailplane.

GULFSTREAM AMERICAN HUSTLER 500

Dimensions: Span, 34 ft 5 in (10,49 m); length, 41 ft 0 in (12,49 m); height, 13 ft 1 in (3,99 m); wing area, 192·76 sq ft (17,90 m²).

IAI KFIR-C2

Country of Origin: Israel.

Type: Single-seat multi-role fighter.

Power Plant: One 11,870 lb (5 385 kg) dry and 17,900 lb (8 120 kg) Bet-Shemesh-built General Electric J79-GE-17 turbojet.

Performance: (Estimated) Max. speed (50% fuel and two Shafrir AAMs), 850 mph (1 368 km/h) at 1,000 ft (305 m) or Mach 1·12, 1,420 mph (2 285 km/h) above 36,000 ft (10 970 m) or Mach 2·3; max. low-level climb rate, 47,250 ft/min (240 m/sec); max. ceiling, 59,050 ft (18 000 m); radius of action (air superiority mission with two 110 Imp gal/500 l drop tanks), 323 mls (520 km), (ground attack mission hi-lo-hi profile), 745 mls (1 200 km).

Weights: Loaded (intercept with 50% fuel and two AAMs), 20,700 lb (9 390 kg); max. take-off, 32,190 lb (14 600 kg).

Armament: Two 30-mm DEFA cannon with 125 rpg and (intercept) two or four Rafael Shafrir AAMs, or (ground attack) up to 8,820 lb (4 000 kg) of external ordnance.

Status: Initial production version of Kfir delivered to Israeli air arm from April 1975 with deliveries of improved Kfir-C2 having commenced early in 1977, production rate at the beginning of 1979 reportedly being 2·5 aircraft monthly.

Notes: The Kfir-C2 differs from the initial production Kfir (Young Lion) in having modifications designed primarily to improve combat manoeuvrability, these comprising canard auxiliary surfaces which result in a close-coupled canard configuration not unlike that of the Saab Viggen (see pages 186—187), dog-tooth wing leading-edge extensions and nose strakes. Equipped with a dual-mode ranging radar, the Kfir is based on the Mirage 5 airframe.

IAI KFIR-C2

Dimensions: Span, 26 ft 11½ in (8,22 m); length, 51 ft 0¼ in (15,55 m); height, 13 ft 11½ in (4,25 m); wing area (excluding canard and dogtooth), 375·12 sq ft (34,85 m²).

IAI SEA SCAN WESTWIND

Country of Origin: Israel.

Type: Light coastal patrol and surveillance aircraft.

Power Plant: Two 3,700 lb (1 678 kg) Garrett AiResearch TFE 731-3-1G turbofans.

Performance: Max. speed, 542 mph (871 km/h) at 19,400 ft (5 915 m); econ. cruise, 460 mph (741 km/h) at 41,000 ft (12 495 m); typical mission (low-altitude off-shore recce), 5·5-hr search pattern at 3,000 ft (915 m) at 244 mph (393 km/h) at 115 mls (185 km) from base, (high-altitude maritime recce), 6 hr at 37,000–45,000 ft (11 280–13 715 m) at 460 mph (741 km/h) covering distance of 2,880 mls (4 635 km).

Weights: Typical empty, 10,290 lb (4 667 kg); max. take-off, 22,850 lb (10 365 kg).

Accommodation: Pilot and co-pilot on flight deck and four/ five systems operators according to individual customer requirements in main pressurised cabin.

Status: Three 1123 Westwind light transports (subsequently upgraded to 1124 standard) converted to Sea Scan configuration for Israeli Navy in 1977. Sea Scan version of latest Westwind I business executive transport currently on offer. Westwind production rate of two per month at beginning of 1979 scheduled to rise to three—four monthly during course of year.

Notes: A maritime version of the basic Westwind (see 1976 edition), the Sea Scan has a Litton LASR-2 search radar and Global Navigation's NS-500A VLF navigation system. Forward-looking infrared, low-light-level television, magnetic anomaly detection equipment, and sonobuoy and chaff dispensers may be fitted.

IAI SEA SCAN WESTWIND

Dimensions: Span, 44 ft 9½ in (13,65 m); length, 55 ft 0 in (16,80 m); height, 15 ft 9½ in (4,81 m); wing area, 308·26 sq ft (28,64 m²).

ILYUSHIN IL-38 (MAY)

Country of Origin: USSR.

Type: Long-range maritime patrol aircraft.

Power Plant: Four 4,250 ehp Ivchenko AI-20M turboprops.

Performance: (Estimated) Max. continuous cruise, 400 mph (645 km/h) at 15,000 ft (4 570 m); normal cruise, 370 mph (595 km/h) at 26,250 ft (8 000 m); patrol speed, 250 mph (400 km/h) at 2,000 ft (610 m); max. range, 4,500 mls (7 240 km); loiter endurance, 12 hrs at 2,000 ft (610 m).

Weights: (Estimated) Empty equipped, 80,000 lb (36 287 kg); max. take-off, 140,000 lb (63 500 kg).

Armament: Internal weapons bay for depth bombs, homing torpedoes, etc. Wing hardpoints for external ordnance loads.

Accommodation: Normal flight crew believed to consist of 12 members, of which half are housed by tactical compartment, operating sensors and co-ordinating data flow to surface vessels and other aircraft.

Status: The Il-38 reportedly flew in prototype form during 1967–68, entering service with the Soviet naval air arm early in 1970. Delivery of three for use by Indian Naval Aviation effected during second half of 1977, and procurement of additional two-three anticipated.

Notes: The Il-38 is a derivative of the Il-18 commercial transport, with essentially similar wings, tail surfaces, engines and undercarriage. By comparison, the wing is positioned further forward on the fuselage for CG reasons. A further military derivative of the Il-18 (known as Coot-A) is utilised for electronic surveillance tasks and features a large canoe-shaped pod beneath the forward fuselage. Unlike the Il-38, the wing positioning of this model is unchanged by comparison with the commercial Il-18.

ILYUSHIN IL-38 (MAY)

Dimensions: Span, 122 ft 9 in (37,40 m); length, 131 ft 0 in (39,92 m); height, 33 ft 4 in (10,17 m); wing area, 1,507 sq ft (140,0 m²).

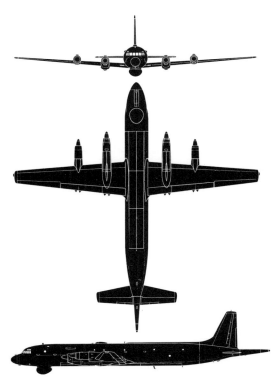

ILYUSHIN IL-76T (CANDID)

Country of Origin: USSR.

Type: Heavy commercial and military freighter.

Power Plant: Four 26,455 lb (12 000 kg) Soloviev D-30KP turbofans.

Performance: Max. cruise, 497 mph (800 km/h) at 29,530 ft (9 000 m); range cruise, 466 mph (750 km/h) at 39,370 ft (12 000 m); max. range (with reserves), 4,163 mls (6 700 km); range with max. payload (88,185 lb/40 000 kg), 3,107 mls (5 000 km).

Weights: Max. take-off, 374,790 lb (170 000 kg).

Accommodation: Normal flight crew of four with navigator below flight deck in glazed nose. Pressurised hold for containerised and other freight, wheeled and tracked vehicles, etc. Military version has pressurised tail station for sighting 23-mm cannon barbette.

Status: First of four prototypes flown on March 25, 1971, with production deliveries to Soviet Air Force commencing 1974, and to Aeroflot (Il-76T) 1976. Export deliveries began in 1978, the Iraqi Air Force being the first recipient.

Notes: The Il-76 is being manufactured in both commercial and military versions, the former (Il-76T) being illustrated above and the latter on opposite page. The current production Il-76 has some 20% more fuel capacity than the initial version and a 1,056-mile (1 700-km) range increase, max. take-off weight having been increased by 28,660 lb (13 000 kg). A flight refuelling tanker version of the Il-76 has been developed for the Soviet Air Force, and the aircraft possesses outstanding short-field capability and may be operated from unprepared airstrips, having a multi-wheel undercarriage with variable-pressure tyres.

ILYUSHIN IL-76T (CANDID)

Dimensions: Span, 165 ft 8⅓ in (50,50 m); length, 152 ft 10¼ in (46,59 m); height, 48 ft 5⅛ in (14,76 m); wing area, 3,229·2 sq ft (300,00 m²).

ILYUSHIN IL-86 (CAMBER)

Country of Origin: USSR.

Type: Medium-haul commercial transport.

Power Plant: Four 28,660 lb (13 000 kg) Kuznetsov NK-86 turbofans.

Performance: Max. cruise, 590 mph (950 km/h) at 29,530 ft (9 000 m); long-range cruise, 559 mph (900 km/h) at 36,090 ft (11 000 m); range (with max. playload—350 passengers), 2,485 mls (4 000 km), (with 250 passengers), 3,107 mls (5 000 km).

Weights: Max. take-off, 454,150 lb (206 000 kg).

Accommodation: Standard flight crew of three—four and up to 350 passengers in basic nine-abreast seating with two aisles (divided between three cabins accommodating 111, 141 and 98 passengers respectively).

Status: First prototype flown on December 22, 1976, and production prototype flown on October 24, 1977. Service entry (with Aeroflot) is scheduled for 1979, and production is a collaborative effort with Polish WSK-Mielec concern (complete stabiliser, all movable aerodynamic surfaces and engine pylons, and the entire wing will be built in Poland from 1980).

Notes: The first wide-body airliner of Soviet design, the Il-86 has been evolved under the supervision of General Designer G. V. Novozhilov and is intended for use on both domestic and international high-density routes. Four are to be supplied to LOT Polish Airlines in 1979–80 in barter for the initial sub-contracts in the IL-86 programme undertaken by WSK-Mielec. A long-haul version of the Il-86 was envisaged with imported General Electric CF6-50 turbofans, but negotiations for the importation of these engines into the Soviet Union broke down in 1978, and the current lack of suitable Soviet engines would suggest that the long-haul project has now been shelved.

ILYUSHIN IL-86 (CAMBER)

Dimensions: Span, 157 ft 8⅛ in (48,06 m); length, 195 ft 4 in (59,54 m); height, 51 ft 10½ in (15,81 m); wing area, 3,550 sq ft (329,80 m²).

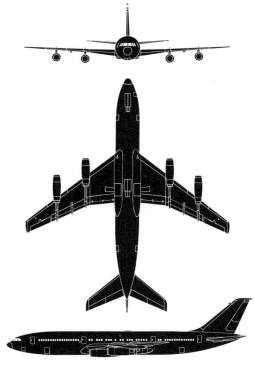

LOCKHEED L-1011-500 TRISTAR

Country of Origin: USA.

Type: Long-haul commercial transport.

Power Plant: Three 48,000 lb (21 772 kg) Rolls-Royce RB.211-524B turbofans.

Performance: (Estimated) Max. cruise, 608 mph (978 km/h) at 31,000 ft (9 450 m); econ. cruise, 567 mph (913 km/h) at 31,000 ft (9 450 m), or Mach 0·84; range (with full passenger payload), 6,053 mls (9 742 km), (with space limited max. payload), 4,855 mls (7 815 km).

Weights: Operational empty, 240,139 lb (108 925 kg); max. take-off, 496,000 lb (224 982 kg).

Accommodation: Basic flight crew of three and mixed-class arrangement for 222 economy (nine-abreast seating) and 24 first (six-abreast seating) class passengers.

Status: First L-1011-500 (for British Airways) flown on October 16, 1978, with delivery scheduled for April 1979, this version of the TriStar also having been ordered by AeroPeru, BWIA, Pan American and Delta. Total of 193 (all versions) on order at beginning of 1979, when production rate was 1·2 monthly, rising to 1·8 monthly by 1980.

Notes: The TriStar 500 is a shorter-fuselage longer-range derivative of the basic L-1011-1 transcontinental version of the TriStar, a 62-in (157,5-cm) section being removed from the fuselage aft of the wing and a 100-in (254-cm) section forward. Versions with the standard fuselage are the L-1011-1, -100 and -200, the last-mentioned model (see 1977 edition) featuring additional centre section fuel tankage and -524 in place of -22B or -22F engines of 42,000 (19 050 kg) and 43,500 lb (19 730 kg) respectively. The -400 is version similar to the -500 but with the -1 wing and smaller engines.

LOCKHEED L-1011-500 TRISTAR

Dimensions: Span, 155 ft 4 in (47,34 m); length, 164 ft 2 in (50,04 m); height, 55 ft 4 in (16,87 m); wing area, 3,456 sq ft (320,00 m²).

LOCKHEED C-130 HERCULES

Country of Origin: USA.

Type: Medium- to long-range military transport.

Power Plant: Four 4,050 eshp Allison T56-A-7A turboprops.

Performance: (C-130H) Max. speed, 384 mph (618 km/h); max. cruise, 368 mph (592 km/h); econ. cruise, 340 mph (547 km/h); range (with max. payload and 5% plus 30 min reserves), 2,450 mls (3 943 km); max. range, 4,770 mls (7 675 km); initial climb, 1,900 ft/min (9,65 m/sec).

Weights: (C-130H) Empty equipped, 72,892 lb (33 063 kg); max. normal take-off, 155,000 lb (70 310 kg); max. overload, 175,000 lb (79 380 kg).

Accommodation: (C-130H) Flight crew of four and max. of 92 troops, 64 paratroops, or 74 casualty stretchers plus two medical attendants. (C-130K Hercules C Mk. 2) Max. of 128 troops or seven cargo pallets.

Status: The 1,500th Hercules was delivered (to Sudan) on March 13, 1978, this total comprising 998 to US services, 433 to overseas governments and 69 to civil operators. C-130H is the principal current production model.

Notes: In the autumn of 1978, the UK Ministry of Defence announced its decision to initiate a "stretch" programme for 30 of the RAF's Hercules C. Mk. 1 (C-130K) transports (equivalent to the C-130H). These are to have two fuselage plugs totalling 180 in (4,57 m) similar to those of the commercial L-100-30, and a prototype conversion (being undertaken by the parent company) will fly in November 1979, the remaining conversions being undertaken in the UK during 1980–83 by Marshall. The "stretched" Hercules C Mk. 2 for the RAF is illustrated above and opposite.

LOCKHEED C-130 HERCULES

Dimensions (Hercules C Mk. 2) Span, 132 ft 7 in (40,41 m);
length, 112 ft 9 in (34,37 m); height, 38 ft 3 in (11,66 m);
wing area, 1,745 sq ft (162,12 m²).

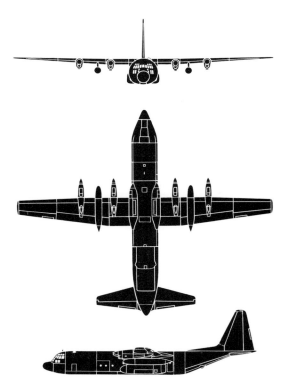

LOCKHEED C-141B STARLIFTER

Country of Origin: USA.

Type: Heavy military strategic transport.

Power Plant: Four 21,000 lb (9 525 kg) Pratt & Whitney TF33-P-7 turbofans.

Performance: Max. cruise, 512 mph (824 km/h) at 38,000 ft (11 590 m), or Mach 0·775; range with max. payload (89,096 lb/44 450 kg), 2,650 mls (4 264 km); max. unrefuelled range (59,800 lb/27 150 kg payload), 4,320 mls (6 950 km).

Weights: Operational empty, 149,904 lb (68 056 kg); max. take-off, 343,000 lb (155 580 kg).

Accommodation: Flight crew of four. Freight hold can accept a total of 13 standard 463L freight pallets totalling 59,800 lb (27 150 kg) in weight.

Status: Sole YC-141B flown on March 24, 1977, and decision announced on June 8, 1978, to convert the USAF's entire fleet of 271 C-141A StarLifters to similar standards as C-141Bs, with the modification programme being scheduled for completion by July 1982.

Notes: The YC-141B is a stretched version of the original C-141A StarLifter, 285 examples of which had been built when production terminated in 1968. The conversion, which increases cargo capability by 35%, comprises stretching the fuselage (in two sections—ahead and aft of the wing) by 23 ft 4 in (7,12 m) and adding drag-reducing fillets at the leading and trailing edges of the wing roots. In addition, flight refuelling capability is incorporated in a fairing aft of the cockpit above the fuselage pressure shell. The flight test programme with the YC-141B was completed in July 1977, two months ahead of schedule. and the C-141B programme is claimed to be the equivalent of adding 90 new transport aircraft to the USAF's inventory.

LOCKHEED YC-141B STARLIFTER

Dimensions: Span, 159 ft 11 in (48,74 m); length, 168 ft 4 in (51,34 m); height, 39 ft 3 in (11,97 m); wing area, 3,228 sq ft (299,90 m²).

LOCKHEED P-3C ORION

Country of Origin: USA.

Type: Long-range maritime patrol aircraft.

Power Plant: Four 4,910 eshp Allison T56-A-14W turbo-props.

Performance: Max. speed at 105,000 lb (47 625 kg), 473 mph (761 km/h) at 15,000 ft (4 570 m); normal cruise, 397 mph (639 km/h) at 25,000 ft (7 620 m); patrol speed, 230 mph (370 km/h) at 1,500 ft (457 m); loiter endurance (all engines) at 1,500 ft (457 m), 12·3 hours, (two engines), 17 hrs; max. mission radius, 2,530 mls (4 075 km), with 3 hrs on station at 1,500 ft (457 m), 1,933 mls (3 110 km); initial climb, 2,880 ft/min (14,6 m/sec).

Weights: Empty, 61,491 lb (27 890 kg); normal max. take-off, 133,500 lb (60 558 kg); max. overload, 142,000 lb (64 410 kg).

Accommodation: Normal flight crew of 10 of which five housed in tactical compartment. Up to 50 combat troops and 4,000 lb (1 814 kg) of equipment for trooping role.

Armament: Weapons bay can house two Mk 101 depth bombs and four Mk 43, 44 or 46 torpedoes, or eight Mk 54 bombs. External ordnance load of up to 13,713 lb (6 220 kg).

Status: YP-3C prototype flown October 8, 1968, P-3C deliveries commencing to US Navy mid-1969 with some 170 by 1979 against planned procurement (through 1982) of 240. Licence manufacture by Kawasaki of 42 (of 45) for Japanese MSDF, six to Iran (as P-3Fs), deliveries of 10 to RAAF continuing into 1979, 18 for Canada (as CP-140 Auroras) from 1980, and 13 for Netherlands from 1981.

LOCKHEED P-3C ORION

Dimensions: Span, 99 ft 8 in (30,37 m); length, 116 ft 10 in (35,61 m); height, 33 ft 8½ in (10,29 m); wing area, 1,300 sq ft (120,77 m²).

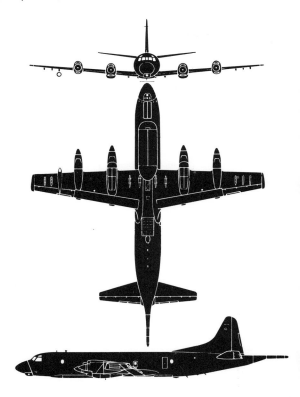

McDONNELL DOUGLAS DC-9 SUPER 80

Country of Origin: USA.

Type: Short- to medium-haul commercial transport.

Power Plant: Two 19,250 lb (8 730 kg) Pratt & Whitney JT8D-209 turbofans (alternative rating of 18,500 lb/8 400 kg).

Performance: Max. cruising speed, 577 mph (928 km/h) at 27,000 ft (8 230 m); long-range cruise, 508 mph (817 km/h) at 35,000 ft (10 670 m); range (with max. payload), 1,508 mls (2 427 km) at 523 mph (841 km/h) at 33,000 ft (10 060 m); max. range (with 22,760 lb/10 324 kg), 3,167 mls (5 095 km) at 508 mph (817 km/h) at 35,000 ft (10 670 m).

Weights: Operational empty, 78,666 lb (35 683 kg); max. take-off, 140,000 lb (63 503 kg).

Accommodation: Flight crew of two and typical mixed-class accommodation for 23 first-class and 137 economy-class passengers, or 155 all economy or 172 commuter-type layouts with five-abreast seating.

Status: The first Super 80 is scheduled to fly in July 1979, with customer deliveries (to Swissair) due to begin March 1980. Approximately 980 DC-9s of all types had been ordered by the beginning of 1979, including more than 40 Super 80s for Pacific Southwest, Austrian, Inex-Adria, Toa, Swissair and Hawaiian.

Notes: The newest and largest member of the DC-9 family with, by comparison with what was previously the largest, the Series 50 (see 1978 edition), a 14 ft 3 in (4,34 m) fuselage "stretch" and an extended wing, larger tailplane, new leading-edge wing slat and uprated engines. A derivative currently being proposed is the Super 80SF combining the wing and engines of the Super 80 with the fuselage of the Series 40 (see 1972 edition).

McDONNELL DOUGLAS DC-9 SUPER 80

Dimensions: Span, 107 ft 10 in (32,85 m); length, 147 ft 10 in (45,08 m); height, 29 ft 4 in (8,93 m); wing area, 1,279 sq ft (118,8 m²).

McDONNELL DOUGLAS DC-10 SERIES 30

Country of Origin: USA.
Type: Medium-range commercial transport.
Power Plant: Three 52,500 lb (23 814 kg) General Electric CF6-50C1 turbofans.
Performance: Max. cruise (at 400,000 lb/181 440 kg), 594 mph (956 km/h) at 31,000 ft (9 450 m); long-range cruise, 540 mph (870 km/h) at 31,000 ft (9 450 m); range (with max. payload), 6,195 mls (9 970 km) at 575 mph (925 km/h) at 31,000 ft (9 450 m); max. range, 7,400 mls (11 910 km) at 540 mph (870 km/h).
Weights: Operational empty, 261,459 lb (118 597 kg); max. take-off, 572,000 lb (259 457 kg).
Accommodation: Flight crew of three plus provision on flight deck for two supernumerary crew. Typical mixed-class accommodation for 225–270 passengers. Max. authorised passenger accommodation, 380 (plus crew of 11).
Status: First DC-10 (Series 10) flown August 29,1970, with first Series 30 (46th DC-10 built) flying June 21, 1972, being preceded on February 28, 1972, by first Series 40. Orders for DC-10s totalled 314 at beginning of 1979, with 41 to be delivered during year and 300th early 1980.
Notes: The DC-10 Series 30 and 40 have identical fuselages to the DC-10 Series 10 (see 1972 edition), but whereas the last-mentioned version is a domestic model, the Series 30 and 40 are intercontinental models and differ in power plant, weights and wing details, and in the use of three main undercarriage units, the third (a twin-wheel unit) being mounted on the fuselage centreline. The Series 40 has 53,000 lb (24 040 kg) Pratt & Whitney JT9D-59A turbofans but is otherwise similar to the Series 30.

McDONNELL DOUGLAS DC-10 SERIES 30

Dimensions: Span, 165 ft 4 in (50,42 m); length, 181 ft 4$\frac{3}{4}$ in (55,29 m); height, 58 ft 0 in (17,68 m); wing area, 3,921·4 sq ft (364,3 m²).

McDONNELL DOUGLAS F-4E PHANTOM

Country of Origin: USA.

Type: Two-seat interceptor and tactical strike fighter.

Power Plant: Two 11,870 lb (5 385 kg) dry and 17,900 lb (8 120 kg) reheat General Electric J79-GE-17 turbojets.

Performance: Max. speed without external stores, 910 mph (1 464 km/h) or Mach 1·2 at 1,000 ft (305 m), 1,500 mph (2 414 km/h) or Mach 2·27 at 40,000 ft (12 190 m); tactical radius (with four·Sparrow III and four Sidewinder AAMs), 140 mls (225 km), (plus one 500 Imp gal/2 273 l auxiliary tank), 196 mls (315 km), (hi-lo-hi mission profile with four 1,000-lb/453,6-kg bombs, four AAMs, and one 500 Imp gal/2 273 l and two 308 Imp gal/1,400 l tanks), 656 mls (1 056 km); max. ferry, 2,300 mls (3 700 km) at 575 mph (925 km/h).

Weights: Empty equipped, 30,425 lb (13 801 kg); loaded (with four Sparrow IIIs), 51,810 lb (21 500 kg), (plus four Sidewinders and max. external fuel), 58,000 lb (26 308 kg); max. overload, 60,630 lb (27 502 kg).

Armament: One 20-mm M-61A1 rotary cannon and (intercept) four or six AIM-7E plus four AIM-9D AAMs, or (attack) up to 16,000 lb (7 257 kg) of external stores.

Status: First F-4E flown June 30, 1967, and production (together with RF-4E) by parent company scheduled to end March 1979, but continuing under licence in Japan (F-4EJ) until 1980, to bring grand total of F-4 production (all versions) to 5,177 aircraft of which 5,039 built by McDonnell Douglas.

Notes: Originally designed as a shipboard fighter and first flown May 27, 1958, the Phantom has been manufactured continuously for 24 years, 1,218 being supplied to the US Navy, 46 to the USMC and 2,640 to the USAF. Foreign operators comprise the UK (F-4K and F-4M), Spain (F-4C), Korea (F-4D and F-4E), Iran (F-4D, F-4E and RF-4E), Germany (RF-4E and F-4F), and Japan, Israel, Greece and Turkey (all operating F-4E and RF-4E).

McDONNELL DOUGLAS F-4E PHANTOM

Dimensions: Span, 38 ft 4¾ in (11,70 m); length, 62 ft 10½ in (19,20 m); height, 16 ft 3⅓ in (4,96 m); wing area, 530 sq ft (49,2 m²).

McDONNELL DOUGLAS AV-8B

Country of Origin: USA.

Type: Single-seat V/STOL strike and reconnaissance fighter.

Power Plant: One 21,500 lb (9 760 kg) Rolls-Royce F402-RR-402 vectored-thrust turbofan.

Performance: (Estimated) Max. speed, 720 mph (1 160 km/h) at 1,000 ft (305 m), or Mach 0·95, (with typical external ordnance), 640 mph (1 030 km/h) at 1,000 ft (305 m), or Mach 0·85; VTO radius (with 1,800-lb/817-kg payload), 230 mls (370 km); STO radius (with 6,000-lb/2 724-kg payload), 460 mls (740 km), (with 2,000-lb/908-kg payload), 920 mls (1 480 km); ferry range, 2,966 mls (4 774 km).

Weights: Operational empty, 12,400 lb (5 265 kg); max. vertical take-off, 18,850 lb (8 558 kg); max. short take-off, 27,950 lb (12 690 kg); max. take-off, 29,550 lb (13 416 kg).

Armament: Two 30-mm cannon in detachable ventral pod as alternative to centreline stores pylon. Seven external pylons (one fuselage and six wing) with combined capacity of 8,000 lb (3 632 kg).

Status: First of two YAV-8Bs (converted from AV-8A Harrier airframes) was flown on November 9, 1978. Full-scale development was scheduled to commence in January 1979, planning calling for construction of four AV-8Bs for 1980—81 trials, with full-scale production commencing in 1983 against US Marine Corps requirement for 336 aircraft.

Notes: The AV-8B is a derivative of the Harrier alias AV-8A (see pages 30—31) with a new graphite epoxy composite wing of supercritical section, redesigned air intakes, various lift improvement devices and new avionics.

McDONNELL DOUGLAS AV-8B

Dimensions: Span, 30 ft 4 in (9,25 m); length, 42 ft 10 in (13,08 m); height, 11 ft 3 in (3,43 m); wing area, 230 sq ft (21,37 m²).

McDONNELL DOUGLAS F-15A EAGLE

Country of Origin: USA.

Type: Single-seat air superiority fighter (F-15A) and two-seat operational trainer (TF-15A).

Power Plant: Two (approx.) 25,000 lb (11 340 kg) reheat Pratt & Whitney F100-PW-100 turbofans.

Performance: Max. speed, 915 mph (1 472 km/h) at sea level or Mach 1·2, 1,650 mph (2 655 km/h) at 36,090 ft (11 000 m) or Mach 2·5; tactical radius (combat air patrol), up to 1,120 mls (1 800 km); ferry range, 2,980 mls (4 800 km), (with Fast Pack auxiliary tanks), 3,450 mls (5 560 km).

Weights: Empty equipped, 26,147 lb (11 860 kg); loaded (clean), 38,250 lb (17 350 kg); max. take-off (intercept mission), 40,000 lb (18 145 kg); max. take-off, 54,123 lb (24 550 kg).

Armament: One 20-mm M-61A-1 rotary cannon with 950 rounds and (intercept mission) four AIM-9L Sidewinder and four AIM-7F Sparrow AAMs. Five stores stations (four wing and one fuselage) can lift up to 15,000 lb (6 804 kg) of ordnance.

Status: First of 20 (18 F-15As and two F-15Bs) flown July 27, 1972, with 606 ordered (including FY 1979) against planned USAF procurement of 729, more than 300 having been delivered by beginning of 1979 when production rate was 6·5 monthly.

Notes: Every seventh production Eagle is a two-seat F-15B, this version being fully combat-capable, and from 1980 the USAF will receive the single-seat F-15C and two-seat F-15D with upgraded avionics and more internal fuel. Israel has received 25 F-15As with further 15 to be delivered 1981–82, and Saudi Arabia to receive 60 from mid-1981. Japan is to procure 88 F-15Cs and 12 F-15Ds 1980–87.

McDONNELL DOUGLAS F-15A EAGLE

Dimensions: Span, 42 ft 9¾ in (13,05 m); length, 63 ft 9 in (19,43 m); height, 18 ft 5½ in (5,63 m); wing area, 608 sq ft (56,50 m²).

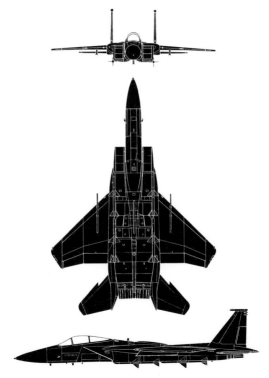

McDONNELL DOUGLAS F-18A HORNET

Country of Origin: USA.

Type: Single-seat shipboard air superiority fighter and attack aircraft.

Power Plant: Two (approx.) 10,600 lb (4 810 kg) dry and 16,000 lb (7 260 kg) reheat General Electric F404-GE-400 turbofans.

Performance: (Estimated) Max. speed, 1,190+ mph (1 915+ km/h) at 36,000 ft (10 970 m) or Mach 1·8+, 915 mph (1 472 km/h) at sea level or Mach 1·2; combat radius (fighter escort mission, internal fuel), 480 mls (770 km), (interdiction mission HI-LO-HI profile with four 1,000-lb/454-kg bombs, two AIM-9 Sidewinders and 1,008 Imp gal/4 584 l external fuel), 670 mls (1 080 km); ferry range, 2,300+ mls (3 700+ km).

Weights: (Estimated) Operational empty, 21,500 lb (9 760 kg); normal loaded (air–air mission, internal fuel), 33,585 lb (15 248 kg); max. take-off, 45,300 lb (20 566 kg).

Armament: One 20-mm multi-barrel M61 cannon and ASMs, bombs, etc, on nine external stations. Max. external load of 19,000 lb (8 618 kg).

Status: First of 11 (nine F-18As and two TF-18As) full-scale development (FSD) aircraft flown November 18, 1978, and remainder scheduled for delivery during course of 1979, in which year production of pilot batch to be initiated. Total requirement of approx. 800 for USN and USMC with anticipated peak production of 11 aircraft monthly in 1985.

Notes: The Hornet is a derivative of the Northrop YF-17 (see 1975 edition), of which McDonnell Douglas is team leader with Northrop being responsible for 30% of airframe development and 40% of airframe production.

McDONNELL DOUGLAS F-18A HORNET

Dimensions: Span (without missiles), 37 ft 6 in (11,43 m); length, 56 ft 0 in (17,07 m); height, 15 ft 4 in (4,67 m); wing area, 400 sq ft (37,16 m²).

MIKOYAN MIG-21BIS (FISHBED-N)

Country of Origin: USSR.

Type: Single-seat multi-role fighter.

Power Plant: One 16,535 lb (7 500 kg) reheat Tumansky R-25 turbojet.

Performance: (Estimated) Max. speed, 808 mph (1 300 km/h) at 1,000 ft (305 m), or Mach 1·06, 1,386 mph (2 230 km/h) above 36,090 ft (11 000 m), or Mach 2·1; tactical radius (intercept mission with centreline drop tank and four K-13A AAMs), 350 mls (560 km); ferry range (max. external fuel), 1,120 mls (1 800 km).

Weights: Approx. normal take-offs (two K-13A missiles and two 108 Imp gal/490 l drop tanks), 20,000 lb (9 070 kg).

Armament: One twin-barrel 23-mm GSh-23 cannon and up to four air-to-air missiles on wing pylons for intercept role. Various external stores for ground attack, including UV-16-57 or UV-32-57 pods containing 16 and 32 55-mm S-5 rockets respectively, 240-mm S-24 rockets or 550-lb (250-kg) bombs.

Status: The MiG-21bis appeared in service with the Soviet Air Forces in 1975 as an upgraded derivative of the MiG-21MF (see 1974 edition).

Notes: The MiG-21bis (Fishbed-N) closely resembles the MiG-21MF (Fishbed-J) externally, but features updated avionics and systems, and introduces an R-25 engine in place of the lower-powered R-13 that powers earlier production versions of the fighter. The MiG-21bis is to be licence-manufactured in India with the production phase-out of the current MiG-21M from 1979. Although still essentially an air combat fighter, the MiG-21bis offers improved ground attack capability.

MIKOYAN MIG-21BIS (FISHED-N)

Dimensions: Span, 23 ft $5\frac{1}{2}$ in (7,15 m); length (including probe), 51 ft $8\frac{1}{2}$ in (15,76 m), (without probe), 44 ft 2 in (13,46 m); wing area, 247·57 sq ft (23,00 m²).

MIKOYAN MIG-23S (FLOGGER-B)

Country of Origin: USSR.
Type: Single-seat interceptor and air superiority fighter.
Power Plant: One 17,635 lb (8 000 kg) dry and 25,350 lb (11 500 kg) reheat Tumansky R-29B turbofan.
Performance: Max. speed, 838 mph (1 350 km/h) at 1,000 ft (305 m) or Mach 1·1, 1,520 mph (2 446 km/h) above 39,370 ft (12 000 m); combat radius (intercept mission with four AAMs and 176 Imp gal/800 l centreline tank), 450–500 mls (725–805 km); max. range (with three 176 Imp gal/800 l drop tanks), 1,400 mls (2 250 km) at 495 mph (795 km/h) or Mach 0·75; ceiling, 60,000 ft (18 300 m).
Weights: Normal loaded (clean), 34,170 lb (15 500 kg); max. take-off, 44,312 lb (20 100 kg).
Armament: One 23-mm twin-barrel GSh-23L cannon plus two AA-7 Apex and two AA-8 Aphid AAMs.
Status: Prototype first flown early 1967 and phased into Soviet Air Force service in intercept and air superiority roles from 1971. Upwards of 1,200 believed in Soviet service by beginning of 1979, when production rate (including MiG-27) was estimated at 500 aircraft per annum.
Notes: Earlier production versions of the MiG-23, including the tandem two-seat MiG-23U (Flogger-C), are powered by the Tumansky R-27 turbofan rated at 15,430 lb (7 000 kg) dry and 22,485 lb (10 200 kg) with maximum reheat, and this power plant is apparently installed in an export model (Flogger-E) which is distinguished by smaller AI radome (housing Jay Bird in place of High Lark radar) and has been supplied to Bulgaria, Cuba, Egypt, Ethiopia, Iraq, Libya and Syria. The MiG-23S was entering Czechoslovak service during 1978.

MIKOYAN MIG-23S (FLOGGER-B)

Dimensions: (Estimated) Span (17 deg sweep), 46 ft 9 in (14,25 m), (72 deg sweep), 27 ft 6 in (8,38 m); length (including probe), 55 ft 1½ in (16,80 m); wing area, 293·4 sq ft (27,26 m²).

MIKOYAN MIG-25 (FOXBAT)

Country of Origin: USSR.
Type: Single-seat interceptor fighter (Foxbat-A) and high-altitude reconnaissance aircraft (Foxbat-B).
Power Plant: Two (estimated) 17,640 lb (8 000 kg) dry and 24,250 lb (11 000 kg) reheat Tumansky turbojets.
Performance: (Estimated—Foxbat-A) Max. short-period dash speed, 1,850 mph (2 980 km/h) or Mach 2·8 above 36,000 ft (10 970 m); max. sea level speed, 650 mph (1 045 km/h) or Mach 0·85; mission radius (max. internal fuel), 590 mls (950 km); max. range, 1,240 mls (2 000 km); service ceiling, 72,180 ft (22 000 m).
Weights: Empty, 44,100 lb (20 000 kg); max. take-off, 77,160 lb (35 000 kg).
Armament: Four AA-6 Acrid AAMs (two infra-red homing and two semi-active radar homing).
Status: The MiG-25 commenced its development trials in the mid 'sixties and apparently entered service in the high-altitude intercept role in 1970–71, and in the reconnaissance role in 1972.
Notes: Three operational versions of the MiG-25 are known to exist, comprising a missile-armed high-altitude interceptor (Foxbat-A), a camera- and IR linescan-equipped reconnaissance model (Foxbat-B) and a SLAR (side-looking aircraft radar) equipped reconnaissance model (Foxbat-D). A two-seat conversion training version (Foxbat-C) possesses no operational capability. The Foxbat-B is illustrated above and the Foxbat-A is illustrated opposite.

MIKOYAN MIG-25 (FOXBAT)

Dimensions: Span, 45 ft 11 in (14,00 m); length (including probe), 73 ft 2 in (22,30 m); height, 18 ft 4½ in (5,60 m); wing area, 602·78 sq ft (56,00 m²).

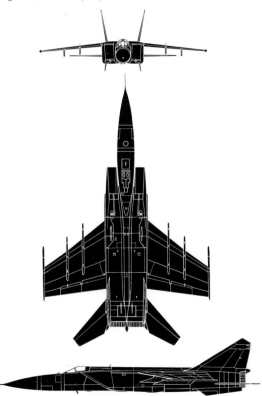

MIKOYAN MIG-27 (FLOGGER-D)

Country of Origin: USSR.

Type: Single-seat tactical strike fighter.

Power Plant: One 17,635 lb (8 000 kg) dry and 25,350 lb (11 500 kg) reheat Tumansky R-29B turbofan.

Performance: Max. speed, 838 mph (1 350 km/h) at 1,000 ft (305 m) or Mach 1·1, 990 mph (1 595 km/h) or Mach 1·5 above 39,370 ft (12 000 m); combat radius (LO-LO-LO mission profile with 176 Imp gal/800 l centreline tank and six 1,102-lb/500-kg bombs), 350 mls (560 km), (HI-LO-HI profile), 550 mls (885 km); max. range (with three 176 Imp gal/800 l drop tanks), 1,400 mls.

Weights: Normal loaded (clean), 34,170 lb (15 500 kg); max. take-off, 44,312 lb (20 100 kg).

Armament: One 23-mm six-barrel rotary cannon and six 1,102-lb (500-kg) bombs, or mix of AS-7 Kerry ASMs, rocket pods and bombs.

Status: A derivative of the MiG-23 interceptor (see pages 156–157), this dedicated tactical strike fighter (also known as MiG-23B) apparently entered Soviet Air Force service in 1974.

Notes: The MiG-27 differs from the MiG-23S primarily in having simple fixed engine air intakes, a drooped forward fuselage to improve ground target acquisition and AI radar deleted in favour of a small radar ranging unit and a laser rangefinder. An export model, the Flogger-F, has been supplied to Algeria, Egypt, Iraq, Libya and Syria.

MIKOYAN MIG-27 (FLOGGER-D)

Dimensions: (Estimated) Span (17 deg sweep), 46 ft 9 in (14,25 m), (72 deg sweep), 27 ft 6 in (8,38 m); length (including probe), 54 ft 0 in (16,46 m); wing area, 293·4 sq ft (27,26 m²).

MITSUBISHI F-1

Country of Origin: Japan.
Type: Single-seat close air support fighter.
Power Plant: Two 4,710 lb (2 136 kg) dry and 7,070 lb (3 207 kg) reheat Ishikawajima-Harima TF40-IHI-801A (Rolls-Royce/Turboméca Adour) turbofans.
Performance: Max. speed, 1,056 mph (1 700 km/h) at 40,000 ft (12 190 m), or Mach 1·6; combat radius (internal fuel only plus four Sidewinder AAMs), 173 mls (278 km), lo-lo-lo (with eight 500-lb/226,8-kg bombs and two 180 Imp gal/820 l drop tanks), 218 mls (351 km), hi-lo-hi (with ASM-1 anti-shipping missiles and one 180 Imp gal/820 l drop tank), 346 mls (556 km); max. ferry range, 1,785 mls (2 870 km); max. climb, 35,000 ft/min (177,8 m/sec).
Weights: Operational empty, 14,017 lb (6 358 kg); max. take-off, 30,146 lb (13 674 kg).
Armament: One 20-mm Vulcan JM-61 multi-barrel cannon. Five external stores stations for up to 8,000 lb (3 629 kg) of ordnance. Detachable multiple ejector racks may be fitted for up to 12 500-lb (226,8-kg) bombs. Wingtip attachment points for two or four Sidewinder or Mitsubishi AAM-1 air-to-air missiles. Two Mitsubishi ASM-1 anti-shipping missiles may be carried.
Status: Two prototypes flown on June 3 and 7, 1975, respectively and first production aircraft flown on June 16, 1977. Fifty-nine ordered for Air Self-Defence Force by beginning of 1979, when total procurement of 80 was envisaged to equip three squadrons.

162

MITSUBISHI F-1

Dimensions: Span, 25 ft 10¼ in (7,88 m); length, 58 ft 7 in (17,86 m); height, 14 ft 4¾ in (4,39 m); wing area, 228 sq ft (21,18 m²).

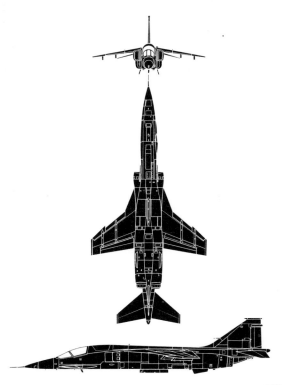

MITSUBISHI MU-300

Country of Origin: Japan.

Type: Light business executive transport.

Power Plant: Two 2,500 lb (1 135 kg) Pratt & Whitney JT15D-4 turbofans.

Performance: (Estimated) Max. cruise, 420–440 mph (675–708 km/h) at 25,000 ft (7 620 m); range cruise, 380–390 mph (610–628 km/h) at 40,000 ft (12 190 m).

Weights: Estimated empty equipped, 7,000 lb (3175 kg); approx. max. take-off, 12,500 lb (5 675 kg).

Accommodation: Normal flight crew of two on separate flight deck and various arrangements for up to nine passengers in main cabin.

Status: Prototype MU-300 was flown on August 29, 1978, and a decision to initiate series production is anticipated during the course of 1979.

Notes: The MU-300 is envisaged as a successor to the turboprop-powered MU-2, emphasis in a low-key development programme having been placed on speed, low noise level, cabin comfort and economy. The prototype MU-300 was expected to be transferred to the USA by early 1979 for FAA certification. If a decision to proceed with production is taken, customer deliveries are likely to commence in 1981.

MITSUBISHI MU-300

Dimensions: (Estimated) Span, 41 ft 0 in (12,50 m); length, 45 ft 0 in (13,70 m); height, 13 ft 0 in (3,95 m).

NORTHROP F-5E TIGER II

Country of Origin: USA.

Type: Single-seat air-superiority fighter.

Power Plant: Two 3,500 lb (1 588 kg) dry and 5,000 lb (2 268 kg) reheat General Electric J85-GE-21 turbojets.

Performance: Max. speed (at 13,220 lb/5 997 kg), 1,056 mph (1 700 km/h) or Mach 1·6 at 36,090 ft (11 000 m), 760 mph (1 223 km/h) or Mach 1·0 at sea level, (with wing-tip missiles), 990 mph (1 594 km/h) or Mach 1·5 at 36,090 ft (11 000 m); combat radius (internal fuel), 173 mls (278 km), (with 229 Imp gal/1 041 l drop tank), 426 mls (686 km); initial climb (at 13,220 lb/5 997 kg), 31,600 ft/min (160,53 m/sec); combat ceiling, 53,500 ft (16 305 m).

Weights: Take-off (wingtip launching rail configuration), 15,400 lb (6 985 kg); max. take-off, 24,083 lb (10 924 kg).

Armament: Two 20-mm M-39 cannon with 280 rpg and two wingtip-mounted AIM-9 Sidewinder AAMs. Up to 7,000 lb (3 175 kg) of ordnance (for attack role).

Status: First F-5E flown August 11, 1972, and first deliveries February 1973. Some 900 (including F-5F) delivered by the beginning of 1979, when production (F-5E and F-5F) was running at 10 per month against orders totalling in excess of 1,100 aircraft.

Notes: A more powerful derivative of the F-5A (see 1970 edition) optimised for the air-superiority role, the F-5E won the USAF's International Fighter Aircraft (IFA) contest in November 1970, and is being supplied under the Military Assistance Programme to South Korea, Taiwan, Thailand and Jordan. Orders for the F-5E have also been placed by eight other air forces, small numbers having also been supplied to the USAF and US Navy. The first two-seat F-5F flew on September 25, 1974, and production deliveries of this version began mid-1976. The F-5E may be fitted with a camera nose.

NORTHROP F-5E TIGER II

Dimensions: Span, 26 ft 8½ in (8,14 m); length, 48 ft 2½ in
(14,69 m); height, 13 ft 4 in (4,06 m); wing area, 186·2
sq ft (17,29 m²).

PANAVIA TORNADO F MK. 2

Country of Origin: United Kingdom.
Type: Two-seat air defence fighter.
Power Plant: Two (approx.) 9,000 lb (4 080 kg) dry and 16,000 lb (7 260 kg) reheat Turbo-Union RB. 199 Mk. 102 turbofans.
Performance: (Estimated) Max. speed (clean), 840 mph (1 350 km/h) at 500 ft (150 m) or Mach 1·1, 1,385 mph (2 230 km/h) at 36,090 ft (11 000 m) or Mach 2·1; typical mission (with two 264 Imp gal/1 200 l external tanks), loiter for 2·0–2·5 hrs plus 10 min combat at distance of 250–450 mls (560–725 km) from base.
Weights: Take-off (with four Sky Flash and two Sidewinder AAMs, plus two 264 Imp gal/1 200 l external tanks), 52,000 lb (23 587 kg).
Armament: One 27-mm Mauser cannon, two AIM-9L Sidewinder AAMs (on pivoting wing pylons) and four Sky Flash AAMs on paired and staggered fuselage pylons.
Status: First of three prototype F Mk. 2s scheduled to fly September–October 1979, with second and third early 1980. RAF requirement for 165 aircraft with service entry commencing 1983.
Notes: The Tornado F Mk. 2 is a UK-only derivative of the multi-national (UK, Federal Germany and Italy) multi-role fighter (see 1978 edition) from which it differs primarily in having Foxhunter intercept radar, uprated engines, 1,400 lb (635 kg) more fuel in a lengthened (by insert of 28 in/71,12 cm) fuselage and a retractable air-to-air refuelling probe replacing the starboard 27-mm cannon. It retains 80% commonality with the multi-role version which is scheduled to enter RAF service (as the G.R. Mk. 1) from late 1979.

PANAVIA TORNADO F MK. 2

Dimensions: Span (max.), 45 ft 8 in (13,90 m), (min.), 28 ft 3 in (8,60 m); length, 58 ft 9 in (17,90 m); height, 18 ft 8½ in (5,70 m); wing area, 322·9 sq ft (30,00 m²).

PILATUS PC-7 TURBO TRAINER

Country of Origin: Switzerland.
Type: Tandem two-seat basic trainer.
Power Plant: One 550 shp (flat rated from 650 shp) Pratt & Whitney PT6A-25A turboprop.
Performance: (At 4,189 lb/1 900 kg) Max. speed, 239 mph (385 km/h) at sea level, 264 mph (425 km/h) at 16,405 ft (5 000 m); cruise, 186 mph (300 km/h) at sea level, 205 mph (330 km/h) at 16,405 ft (5 000 m); max. range (at 40% power with 5% plus 20 min reserve), 777 mls (1 250 km); initial climb, 2,008 ft/min (10,2 m/sec).
Weights: Empty, 2,866 lb (1 300 kg); max. take-off (clean), 4,189 lb (1 900 kg), (external stores), 5,952 lb (2 700 kg).
Armament: Six wing hardpoints permit external loads of ordnance and other stores up to maximum of 5,952 lb (2 700 kg).
Status: First of two PC-7 prototypes flown on April 12, 1966, and first production example flown July 1978. Initial production batch of 35 commenced in 1977, with production rate of two—three per month at beginning of 1979 scheduled to rise to four—five monthly by mid-year and second production batch (40 aircraft) laid down.
Notes: Derived from the piston-engined PC-3, the PC-7 has been ordered by Bolivia, Burma and Mexico, and is expected to replace the PC-3 in Swiss Air Force service from the mid-'eighties onwards, Swiss procurement of 60 aircraft being envisaged. Marketing collaboration is being provided by Dornier GmbH of Germany.

PILATUS PC-7 TURBO TRAINER

Dimensions: Span, 34 ft 1½ in (10,40 m); length, 31 ft 11⅞ in (9,75 m); height, 10 ft 6⅓ in (3,21 m); wing area, 178·68 sq ft (16,60 m²).

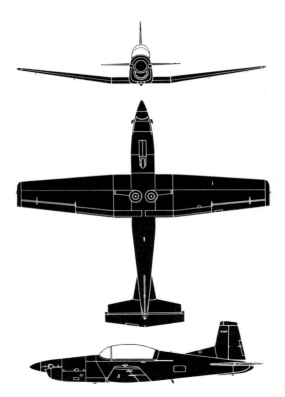

PIPER PA 38 TOMAHAWK

Country of Origin: USA.

Type: Side-by-side two-seat primary trainer.

Power Plant: One 112 bhp Avco Lycoming 0-235-L2C four-cylinder horizontally-opposed engine.

Performance: Max. speed, 130 mph (209 km/h) at sea level; cruise (75% power), 125 mph (202 km/h) at 8,800 ft (2 680 m), (65% power), 117 mph (189 km/h) at 11,500 ft (3 505 m); range (with 45 min reserve), 463 mls (745 km) at 75% power, 500 mls (807 km) at 65% power; initial climb, 700 ft/min (3,55 m/sec); service ceiling, 12,850 ft (3 917 m).

Weights: Empty equipped, 1,064 lb (483 kg); max. take-off, 1,670 lb (757 kg).

Status: The PA-38 Tomahawk trainer was announced in October 1977, and customer deliveries commenced early in 1978, more than 1,000 having been delivered by the beginning of 1979, when production exceeded 100 monthly.

Notes: Placing emphasis on simplicity of maintenance and low operating costs, the Tomahawk incorporates a high degree of component interchangeability and several design features considered innovative in aircraft of its category. Like the Beechcraft Skipper (see pages 42–43), with which the new Piper trainer is directly competitive, the Tomahawk employs a T-tail, which is claimed to afford greater stability and more positive rudder control, and its high aspect ratio wing of constant chord and thickness utilises a NASA Whitcomb aerofoil.

PIPER PA 38 TOMAHAWK

Dimensions: Span, 34 ft 0 in (10,36 m); length, 23 ft 1¼ in (7,04 m); height, 8 ft 7½ in (2,63 m); wing area, 125 sq ft (11,61 m²).

PIPER PA-42 CHEYENNE IIIT

Country of Origin: USA.

Type: Light business executive transport.

Power Plant: Two 680 shp (de-rated from 850 shp) Pratt & Whitney (Canada) PT6A-41 turboprops.

Performance: Max. cruise, 330 mph (532 km/h) at 15,000 ft (4 570 m), 347 mph (558 km/h) at 20,000 ft (6 095 m); max. range, 1,658 mls (2 668 km) at 15,000 ft (4 570 m), 1,968 mls (3 167 km) at 25,000 ft (7 620 m); initial climb, 2,450 ft/min (12,44 m/sec); service ceiling, 30,500 ft (9 295 m).

Weights: Empty equipped, 5,621 lb (2 550 kg); max. take-off, 10,550 lb (4 785 kg).

Accommodation: Flight crew of one or two on separate flight deck with six–ten passengers in main cabin.

Status: First production PA-42 flown mid-1978, customer deliveries having been delayed until mid-1979 to permit introduction of 36-in (91,44 cm) fuselage "stretch".

Notes: The original PA-31T Cheyenne prototype flew on August 20, 1969, with customer deliveries commencing in 1974, this initial model currently being offered as the Cheyenne I with 500 shp PT6A-11s and as the Cheyenne II with 620 shp PT6A-28s. The PA-42 Cheyenne IIIT is an extensively redesigned model with more powerful engines, enlarged overall dimensions and a tail of the increasingly fashionable T-type.

174

PIPER PA-42 CHEYENNE IIIT

Dimensions: Span, 47 ft 8⅛ in (14,53 m) length, 41 ft 0 in (12,50 m); height, 11 ft 9½ in (3,61 m); wing area, 293 sq ft (27,20 m²).

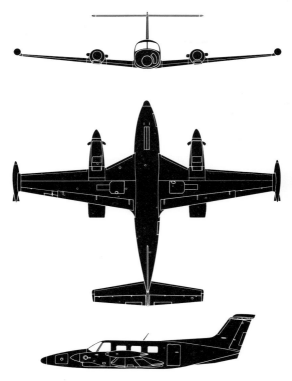

PIPER PA-44 SEMINOLE

Country of Origin: USA.

Type: Light cabin monoplane.

Power Plant: Two 180 hp Avco Lycoming 0-360-E1AD four-cylinder horizontally-opposed engines.

Performance: Max. speed, 192 mph (309 km/h) at sea level; cruise (75% power), 186 mph (300 km/h), (65% power), 178 mph (286 km/h), (55% power), 170 mph (273 km/h); range (with 45 min reserve), 820 mls (1 321 km) at 75% power, 890 mls (1 435 km) at 65% power, 960 mls (1 546 km) at 55% power; initial climb, 1,220 ft/min (6,2 m/sec); service ceiling, 16,000 ft (4 875 m).

Weights: Empty, 2,406 lb (1 091 kg); max. take-off, 3,800 lb (1 723 kg).

Accommodation: Pilot and three passengers in individual seats and baggage compartment of 24 cu ft (0.68 m³) capacity.

Status: The prototype PA-44 Seminole flew in May 1976, and initial production deliveries commenced two years later, in May 1978, with more than 140 planned for delivery by the beginning of 1979.

Notes: An all-new design intended as a twin-engined trainer for pilots who have previously flown only single-engined aircraft, the Seminole closely resembles the Duchess 76 (see pages 40–41).

176

PIPER PA-44 SEMINOLE

Dimensions: Span, 38 ft 6½ in (11,75 m); length, 27 ft 7 in (8,41 m); height, 8 ft 6 in (2,59 m).

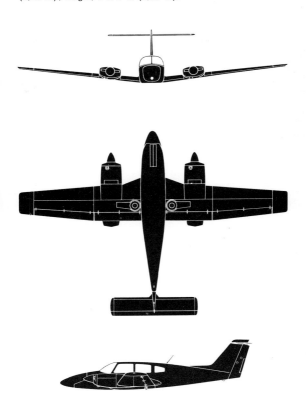

PZL-M-15 BELPHEGOR

Country of Origin: Poland.
Type: Single-seat agricultural aircraft.
Power Plant: One 3,307 lb (1 500 kg) Ivchenko AI-25 turbofan.
Performance: Max. cruise, 124 mph (200 km/h); normal operating speeds, 87–102 mph (140–165 km/h); endurance, 1·5 hrs (plus 30 min reserve); initial climb, 1,083 ft/min (5,5 m/sec).
Weights: Empty equipped, 6,393 lb (2 900 kg); max. take-off, 12,456 lb (5 650 kg).
Status: Aerodynamic prototype (LLP-M15) flown May 20, 1973, followed by first representative prototype on January 9, 1974. First batch of five of initial pre-production batch of 20 aircraft delivered to USSR for trials on April 26, 1975, and production at a rate of 40–60 annually for export to the Soviet Union was continuing at the beginning of 1979.
Notes: The M-15 is unique in being the world's only turbofan-powered biplane. It is also one of the largest agricultural aircraft so far produced, the containers between the wings having a combined capacity of 4,850 lb (2 200 kg) of dry chemicals or 638 Imp gal (2 900 l) of liquid chemicals. The M-15 was evolved by a joint Polish-Soviet design team under the leadership of Kazimierz Gocyla to the requirements of a specification drawn up by the Soviet Ministry of Civil Aviation, and all production is currently being undertaken against orders from the USSR. Choice of biplane configuration was dictated by the need to maintain a low wing loading such as was demanded by the working speed despite a high take-off weight.

PZL-M-15 BELPHEGOR

Dimensions: Span, 73 ft 3⅛ in (22,33 m); length, 41 ft 8¾ in (12,72 m); height, 17 ft 6½ in (5,34 m); wing area, 723·33 sq ft (67,20 m²).

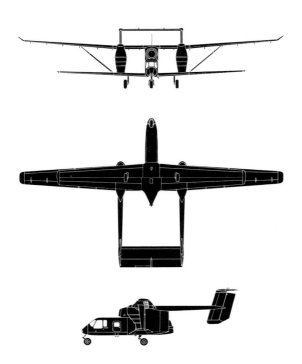

RFB FANTRAINER ATI-2

Country of Origin: Federal Germany.
Type: Tandem two-seat basic trainer.
Power Plant: One 420 shp Allison 250-C2OB turboshaft engine driving a ducted fan.
Performance: (Estimated) Max. speed, 224 mph (360 km/h) at sea level; max. cruise, 199 mph (320 km/h); max. climb rate, 1,968 ft/min (10 m/sec); max. range, 684 mls (1 100 km).
Weights: Empty, 1,984 lb (900 kg); max. take-off, 3,482 lb (1 580 kg).
Status: First prototype (D1) flown on October 27, 1977, with second prototype (D2) following on May 31, 1978.
Notes: The Fantrainer utilises an integrated ducted-fan propulsion system, which, while simulating the characteristics of a pure turbojet, offers appreciably lower operating costs. The Fantrainer is intended to cover all phases of the training spectrum up to relatively advanced types such as the Alpha Jet, and the first prototype (D1) employs two coupled Audi-NSU Wankel rotating piston engines, each of 150 hp, while the second prototype (the D2 described and illustrated) is powered by a single turboshaft. Late in 1978, the Fantrainer D2 was evaluated by the *Luftwaffe* as a standard primary-basic trainer, the other contenders being the more conventional Pilatus PC-7 and Beech T-34C.

RFB FANTRAINER ATI-2

Dimensions: Span, 31 ft 5$\frac{7}{8}$ in (9,60 m); length, 29 ft 4$\frac{1}{3}$ in (8,95 m); height, 9 ft 6$\frac{1}{8}$ in (2,90 m); wing area, 149·6 sq ft (13,90 m²).

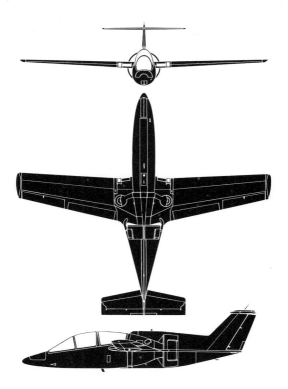

ROCKWELL (FUJI) COMMANDER 700

Countries of Origin: USA and Japan.

Type: Light cabin monoplane.

Power Plant: Two 340 hp Avco Lycoming TIO-540-R2AD six-cylinder horizontally-opposed engines.

Performance: Max. speed, 254 mph (409 km/h) at 20,000 ft (6 095 m); cruise (75% power), 251 mph (403 km/h) at 24,000 ft (7 315 m); max. range (45 min reserve), 1,196 mls (1 924 km); initial climb, 1,633 ft/min (8,3 m/sec); service ceiling, 30,000 ft (9 235 m).

Weights: Standard empty, 4,620 lb (2 096 kg); max. take-off, 6,987 lb (3 170 kg).

Accommodation: Pilot and co-pilot/passenger in individual seats with dual controls and various layouts for four passengers (with fifth optional seat) in main pressurised cabin.

Status: The first prototype was flown (in Japan) on November 13, 1975, and the second (in the USA) on February 25, 1976. First customer delivery on August 21, 1978, and total of 14 was scheduled to be delivered by beginning of 1979.

Notes: The Commander 700 (known in Japan as the FA-300) is a joint programme between Rockwell International and Fuji under which the respective participants are responsible for the assembly of all aircraft for sale in their defined marketing areas. Rockwell has ordered 42 Commander 700 shipsets from Fuji for delivery by September 1979, and was scheduled to take a decision concerning further shipsets by January 1979. The Commander 710 (FA-300-KAI), flown (in Japan) on December 22, 1976, has 450 hp engines and first production deliveries are scheduled for September 1979.

ROCKWELL (FUJI) COMMANDER 700

Dimensions: Span, 42 ft 4⅞ in (12,90 m); length, 38 ft 2⅛ in (11,60 m); height, 13 ft 3½ in (4,10 m); wing area, 200·2 sq ft (18,60 m²).

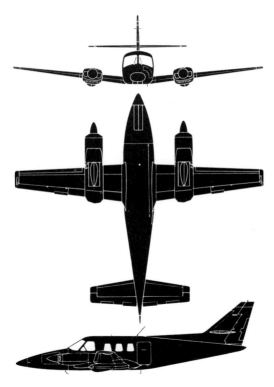

ROCKWELL SABRELINER 65

Country of Origin: USA.

Type: Light business executive transport.

Power Plant: Two 3,700 lb (1 678 kg) Garrett AiResearch TFE 731-3-1D turbofans.

Performance: Max. speed, 528 mph (850 km/h), or Mach 0·8; recommended cruise, 495 mph (796 km/h), or Mach 0·75; long-range cruise, 462 mph (743 km/h), or Mach 0·7; range (four passengers and VFR reserve), 3,328 mls (5 354 km); initial climb, 3,540 ft/min (20 m/sec); cruise altitude, 39,000 ft (11 890 m).

Weights: Empty equipped, 13,330 lb (6 046 kg); max. take-off, 23,800 lb (10 795 kg).

Accommodation: Normal flight crew of two and basic cabin arrangements for seven, eight or ten passengers.

Status: First of three prototype Sabreliner 65s flown June 29, 1977, with customer deliveries scheduled for second half of 1979 at rate of two per month.

Notes: The Sabreliner 65 is a progressive development of the Sabreliner 60 (see 1968 edition) with turbofans and utilising supercritical aerofoil technology, plain flaps being replaced by Fowler-type flaps, spoilers replacing the centreline air brake, an aft fuselage fuel tank being introduced and wing fuel capacity being increased. Similar changes are to be incorporated in the larger Sabreliner 75A (see 1975 edition) and deliveries of this model, to be known as the Sabreliner 80A, are scheduled to commence in December 1979. Further developments include the Sabreliner 85 with a "stretched Sabreliner 75 fuselage, a new supercritical wing and Rolls-Royce RB.401 turbofans for 1982 introduction.

ROCKWELL SABRELINER 65

Dimensions: Span, 50 ft 1 in (15,26 m); length, 46 ft 11 in (14,30 m); height, 16 ft 0 in (4,88 m); wing area, 380 sq ft (35,30 m²).

SAAB (JA) 37 VIGGEN

Country of Origin: Sweden.

Type: Single-seat all-weather intercepter fighter with secondary strike capability.

Power Plant: One 16,203 lb (7 350 kg) dry and 28,108 lb (12 750 kg) reheat Volvo Flygmotor RM 8B.

Performance: (Estimated) Max. speed (with two RB 24 Sidewinder AAMs), 1,320 mph (2 125 km/h) above 36,090 ft (11 000 m) or Mach 2·0, 910 mph (1 465 km/h) at 1,000 ft (305 m) or Mach 1·2; operational radius (M = 2·0 intercept with two AAMs), 250 mls (400 km), (lo-lo-lo ground attack with six Mk. 82 bombs), 300 mls (480 km); time (from brakes off) to 32,810 ft (10 000 m), 1·4 min.

Weights: (Estimated) Empty, 26,895 lb (12 200 kg); loaded (two AAMs), 37,040 lb (16 800 kg); max. take-off, 49,600 lb (22 500 kg).

Armament: One semi-externally mounted 30-mm Oerlikon KCA cannon with 150 rounds and up to 13,227 lb (6 000 kg) of ordnance on seven external stores stations.

Status: First of four JA 37 prototypes (modified from AJ 37 airframes) flown June 1974, with fifth prototype built from outset to JA 37 standards flown December 15, 1975. Initial production JA 37 flown on November 4, 1977. Total of 149 JA 37s (of 329 Viggens of all types) being procured.

Notes: The JA 37 is a development of the AJ 37 (see 1973 edition) which is optimised for the attack role. The JA 37 has uprated turbofan, will carry a mix of BAe Sky Flash AAMs and cannon armament, and has X-Band Pulse Doppler radar.

SAAB (JA) 37 VIGGEN

Dimensions: Span, 34 ft 9¼ in (10,60 m); length (excluding probe), 50 ft 8¼ in (15,45 m); height, 19 ft 4¼ in (5,90 m); wing area (including foreplanes), 561·88 sq ft (52,20 m²).

SEPECAT JAGUAR INTERNATIONAL

Countries of Origin: France and United Kingdom.
Type: Single-seat tactical strike fighter.
Power Plant: Two 5,260 lb (2 386 kg) dry and 8,000 lb (3 630 kg) reheat Rolls-Royce Turboméca RT.172-26 Adour 804 turbofans.
Performance: (At typical weight) Max. speed, 820 mph (1 320 km/h) or Mach 1·1 at 1,000 ft (305 m), 1,057 mph (1 700 km/h) or Mach 1·6 at 32,810 ft (10 000 m); cruise with max. ordnance, 430 mph (690 km/h) or Mach 0·65 at 39,370 ft (12 000 m); range with external fuel for lo-lo-lo mission profile, 450 mls (724 km), for hi-lo-hi mission profile, 710 mls (1 142 km); ferry range, 2,270 mls (3 650 km).
Weights: Normal take-off, 23,000 lb (10 430 kg); max. take-off, 32,600 lb (14 790 kg).
Armament: Two 30-mm Aden cannon and up to 10,000 lb (4 536 kg) ordnance on five external hardpoints.
Status: First of eight Jaguar prototypes flown September 8, 1968, and first production on November 2, 1971. Joint production by Dassault-Breguet and BAe (as SEPECAT) of which RAF orders for 202 Jaguars completed by 1979, together with 154 of 174 ordered for *Armée de l'Air*. Deliveries of 12 Jaguar Internationals for each of Ecuador and Oman completed by mid-1978, and 40 to be delivered to India from early 1979.
Notes: Whereas Jaguars of the RAF and *Armée de l'Air* have Adour 102s of 5,115 lb (2 320 kg) dry and 7,305 lb (3 314 kg) reheat, the export Jaguar International has uprated Adour 804s. Licence production of 110–160 to be undertaken in India.

SEPECAT JAGUAR INTERNATIONAL

Dimensions: Span, 28 ft 6 in (8,69 m); length, 50 ft 11 in (15,52 m); height, 16 ft 0½ in (4,89 m); wing area, 258·33 sq ft (24,00 m²).

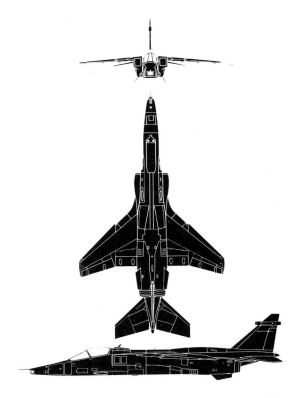

SHORTS 330

Country of Origin: United Kingdom.

Type: Third-level airliner and utility transport.

Power Plant: Two 1,173 shp Pratt & Whitney (Canada) PT6A-45A turboprops.

Performance: Max. cruise, 221 mph (356 km/h) at 10,000 ft (3 050 m); range cruise, 184 mph (296 km/h) at 10,000 ft; range (with 30 passengers and baggage, no reserve), 450 mls (725 km), (typical freighter configuration with 7,500-lb/ 3 400 kg payload), 368 mls (592 km); max range (passenger configuration with 4,060-lb/1 840-kg payload), 1,013 mls (1 630 km), (freighter configuration with 5,400-lb/2 450-kg payload), 1,013 mls (1 630 km); max. climb, 1,210 ft/min (6,14 m/sec).

Weights: Empty equipped (for 30 passengers), 14,500 lb (6 577 kg); max. take-off, 22,400 lb (10 160 kg).

Accommodation: Standard flight crew of two and normal accommodation for 30 passengers in 10 rows three abreast and 1,000 lb (455 kg) of baggage.

Status: Engineering prototype flown August 22, 1974, with production prototype following on July 8, 1975. First production aircraft flown on December 15, 1975. Customer deliveries commenced mid-1976, and at the beginning of 1979, a total of 36 aircraft had been ordered with approximately 22 delivered.

Notes: The Shorts 330 is derived from the Skyvan STOL utility transport (see 1975 edition) and is designed primarily for commuter and regional air service operators. Retaining many of the Skyvan's characteristics, including its large cabin cross section, Shorts 330 had been ordered by 10 operators by the beginning of 1979, and a maritime surveillance version, the SD3-MR Seeker with nose-mounted radar, search-and-rescue equipment, etc, was on offer.

SHORTS 330

Dimensions: Span, 74 ft 8 in (22,76 m); length, 58 ft 0½ in (17,69 m); height, 16 ft 3 in (4,95 m); wing area, 453 sq ft (42,10 m²).

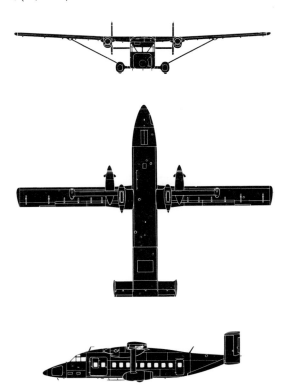

SUKHOI SU-15VD (FLAGON-F)

Country of Origin: USSR.

Type: Single-seat all-weather interceptor fighter.

Power Plant: Two 17,195 lb (7 800 kg) dry and 24,700 lb (11 200 kg) reheat Lyulka AL-21 turbojets.

Performance: (Estimated) Max. speed (clean configuration), 1,650 mph (2 755 km/h) above 36,000 ft (10 970 m), or Mach 2·5, (high drag configuration: e.g., drop tanks on fuselage stations and AA-6 Acrid AAMs on wing stations), 1,120 mph (1 800 km/h), or Mach 1·7; tactical radius (internal fuel), 450 mls (725 km); time to 36,000 ft (10 970 m), 2·5 min.

Weights: (Estimated) Empty equipped, 28,000 lb (12 700 kg); max. take-off, 45,000 lb (20 410 kg).

Armament: Two AA-3 Anab or AA-6 Acrid radar-guided air-to-air missiles on underwing pylons.

Status: The Su-15 apparently flew in prototype form during 1964-65, entering service with the IAP-VO Strany (the fighter element of the Anti-aircraft Defence of the Homeland) in 1969. It has since been progressively developed, the latest known service version being the Su-15VD (Flagon-F).

Notes: The initial production version of the Su-15, the Flagon-A, employed a plain delta wing similar to that of the earlier Su-11 (Fishpot-C), but this gave place on the next production model (Flagon-D) to a wing of extended span employing compound sweep, variants of this being an experimental STOL (short-take-off-and-landing) technology development version featuring three vertical lift jets mounted centrally in the fuselage (Flagon-B) and a tandem two-seat conversion training version (Flagon-C). Further wing modifications were introduced by the next single-seat production model (Flagon-E), and the latest version (Flagon-F), described above and illustrated, has new radar in an ogival rather than conical nose and uprated engines.

SUKHOI SU-15VD (FLAGON-F)

Dimensions: (Estimated) Span, 34 ft 5 in (10,50 m); length, 70 ft 6 in (20,50 m); height, 16 ft 6 in (5,00 m); wing area, 387 sq ft (36,00 m²).

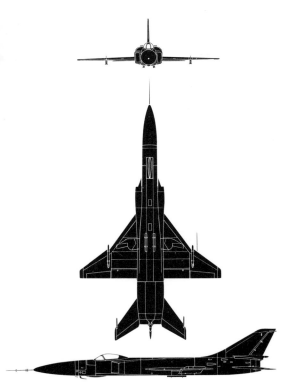

SUKHOI SU-17 (FITTER-C)

Country of Origin: USSR.

Type: Single-seat tactical strike fighter.

Power Plant: One 17,195 lb (7 800 kg) dry and 24,700 lb (11 200 kg) reheat Lyulka AL-21F-3 turbojet.

Performance: Max. speed (clean), 808 mph (1 300 km/h) or Mach 1·06 at sea level, 1,430 mph (2 300 km/h) at 39,370 ft (12 000 m) or Mach 2·17; combat radius (lo-lo-lo mission profile), 260 mls (420 km), (hi-lo-hi mission profile), 373 mls (600 km); range (with 2,205-lb/1 000-kg weapon load and auxiliary fuel), 1,415 mls (2 280 km); service ceiling, 57,415 ft (17 500 m).

Weights: Max. take-off, 39,022 lb (17 700 kg).

Armament: Two 30-mm NR-30 cannon with 70 rpg and (for short-range missions) a max. external ordnance load of 7,716 lb (3 500 kg). Typical external stores include UV-16-57 or UV-32-57 rocket pods containing 16 and 32 55-mm S-5 rockets respectively, 240-mm S-24 rockets, two AS-7 Kerry ASMs, or 550-lb (250-kg) or 1,100-lb (500-kg) bombs.

Status: The Su-17 entered service with the Soviet Air Forces in 1972, and has been exported to Algeria, Czechoslovakia, Egypt, Iraq, Libya, Poland and Syria.

Notes: The Su-17 is a variable-geometry derivative of the Su-7 Fitter-A (see 1973 edition). Intended primarily for the close air support, battlefield interdiction and counterair roles, but with secondary combat zone air superiority capability, the Su-17 has been offered for export under the designations Su-20 and Su-22 (the latter being purchased by Peru), these differing in equipment standards, and the latest variant (Fitter-D) has a laser target seeker in a housing beneath the nose.

SUKHOI SU-17 (FITTER-C)

Estimated Dimensions: Span (max.), 45 ft 0 in (13,70 m), (min.), 32 ft 6 in (9,90 m); length (including probe), 57 ft 0 in (17,37 m); height, 15 ft 5 in (4,70 m).

SUKHOI SU-19 (FENCER-A)

Country of Origin: USSR.

Type: Two-seat ground attack fighter.

Power Plant: Two 17,635 lb (8 000 kg) dry and 25,350 lb (11 500 kg) reheat Tumansky R-29B turbofans.

Performance: (Estimated) Max. speed, 760–840 mph (1 225–1 350 km/h) at sea level or Mach 1·0–1·1, 1,385–1,520 mph (2 230–2 445 km/h) at 36,090 ft (11 000 m) or Mach 2·1–2·3; radius of action (lo-lo-lo), 250 mls (400 km), (hi-lo-hi), 750 mls (1 200 km); max. endurance, 3–4 hrs.

Weights: (Estimated) Empty equipped, 33,000 lb (14 970 kg); max. take-off, 68,000 lb (30 845 kg).

Armament: One six-barrel 23-mm rotary cannon in the underside of the fuselage and up to 10,000–11,000 lb (4 500–5 000 kg) of ordnance on six external stations (two under the fuselage and four under the fixed wing glove), a typical ordnance load comprising two 1,100-lb (500-kg) bombs, two surface-to-air missiles and two pods each containing 16 or 32 57-mm unguided rockets.

Status: Prototypes of the Su-19 are believed to have flown in 1970, and this type was first reported to be in service with the Soviet Air Forces during the course of 1974. Western intelligence agencies indicated that some 250 will have attained service by mid-1979.

Notes: The Su-19 (the accompanying illustrations of which should be considered as provisional) is the first Soviet fighter optimised for the ground attack role to have achieved service status. Wing leading-edge sweep varies from approximately 23 deg fully spread to 70 deg fully swept, and the wings reportedly incorporate both leading- and trailing-edge lift devices and lift dumpers acting as spoilers in conjunction with differential tailplane movement for roll control.

SUKHOI SU-19 (FENCER-A)

Dimensions: (Estimated) Span (max.), 56 ft 0 in (17,00 m), (min.), 31 ft 0 in (9,45 m); length, 70 ft 0 in (21,25 m); height, 18 ft 0 in (5,50 m); wing area, 409 sq ft (38,00 m²).

TRANSALL C-160

Countries of Origin: France and Federal Germany.
Type: Medium-range tactical transport.
Power Plant: Two 6,100 ehp Rolls-Royce Tyne RTy 20 Mk. 22 turboprops.
Performance: (At 112,435 lb/51 000 kg) Max. speed, 322 mph (518 km/h) at 16,000 ft (4 875 m); econ. cruise, 282 mph (454 km/h) at 20,000 ft (6 100 m); range (with 35,274-lb/16 000-kg payload), (1,150 mls (1,850 km), (with 17,640-lb/8 000-kg payload), 3,170 mls (5 100 km), (with 6,614-lb/3 000-kg payload), 4,350 mls (7 000 km); ferry range, 5,500 mls (8 850 km); max. initial climb, 1,300 ft/min (6,6 m/sec); service ceiling, 25,500 ft (7 770 m).
Weights: Min. operational empty, 61,730 lb (28 000 kg); max. take-off, 112,435 lb (51 000 kg).
Accommodation: Crew of four and 62–88 paratroops, max. of 93 fully-equipped troops, up to 63 casualty stretchers and four medical attendants, or loads up to 37,500 lb (17 000 kg).
Status: First prototype flown February 25, 1963, and two further prototypes and 179 production aircraft built by time series manufacture terminated in 1972. Production resumed in 1978 against requirement for further 25 aircraft for *Armée de l'Air* and three for *Postale de Nuit,* with deliveries to commence 1981. Production being shared equally between France (Aéro-spatiale) and Germany (MBB and VFW-Fokker). Twelve had been funded by the beginning of 1979.
Notes: New series will have centre-section fuel tanks and will also be fitted as in-flight tankers and receivers.

TRANSALL C-160

Dimensions: Span, 131 ft 3 in (40,00 m); length, 106 ft 4 in (32,40 m); height, 38 ft 3 in (11,65 m); wing area, 1,722 sq ft (160 m²).

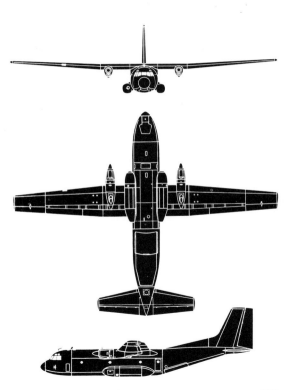

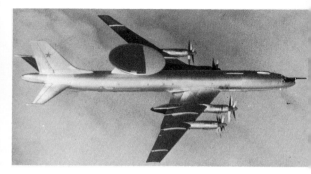

TUPOLEV TU-126 (MOSS)

Country of Origin: USSR.

Type: Airborne warning and control system aircraft.

Power Plant: Four 14,795 ehp Kuznetsov NK-12MV turbo-props.

Performance: (Estimated) Max. speed, 510 mph (820 km/h); max. continuous cruise, 460 mph (740 km/h) at 25,000 ft (7 620 m); operational cruise, 410 mph (660 km/h) at 21,325 ft (6 500 m); mission endurance (unrefuelled), 9 hrs at 620-mile (1 000-km) radius, 6 hrs at 1,240-mile (2 000-km) radius; service ceiling, 36,090 ft (11 000 m).

Weights: (Estimated) Normal max. take-off, 360,000 lb (163,290 kg).

Status: The Tu-126 AWACS aircraft is believed to have flown in prototype form in 1962–63 and first appeared in service with the Soviet Air Forces in the late 'sixties. Some 20–30 aircraft of this type are believed to be in service.

Notes: Essentially an adaptation of the Tu-114 commercial transport and retaining basically similar wings, tail surfaces power plant and undercarriage to those of the earlier aircraft, the Tu-126 is primarily intended to locate low-flying intruders and to vector interceptors towards them. The dominating feature of the aircraft is its pylon-mounted saucer-shaped early-warning scanner. The Tu-126 reportedly operates most effectively over water, possessing only limited overland "look-down" capability.

TUPOLEV TU-126 (MOSS)

Dimensions: Span, 168 ft 0 in (51,20 m); approx. length, 188 ft 0 in (57,30 m); height, 51 ft 0 in (15,50 m); wing area, 3,349 sq ft (311,1 m²).

TUPOLEV TU-144 (CHARGER)

Country of Origin: USSR.
Type: Long-range supersonic commercial transport.
Power Plant: Four 33,100 lb (15 000 kg) dry and 44,090 lb (20 000 kg) reheat Kuznetsov NK-144 turbofans.
Performance: Max. cruise, 1,550 mph (2 500 km/h) at altitudes up to 59,000 ft (18 000 m), or Mach 2·3; long-range cruise, 1,254 mph (2,018 km/h) at 52,490—55,775 ft (16 000—17 000 m), or Mach 1·9; max. range, 4,040 mls (6 500 km).
Weights: Operational empty, 187,395 lb (85 000 kg); max. take-off, 396,830 lb (180 000 kg).
Accommodation: Basic flight crew of three and maximum of 140 passengers in single-class arrangement with three-plus-two and two-plus-two seating.
Status: First pre-production aircraft (representative of production configuration) flown September 1971, and total of 20 (including pre-production aircraft) had reportedly been completed by early 1979.
Notes: Technical problems, reportedly including excessive fuel consumption during cruise with partial reheat, delayed the introduction of the Tu-144 on regular passenger services until November 1, 1977, when Aeroflot initiated a regular service between Moscow and Alma Ata, mail and cargo flights having been made over this 2,190-mile (3 520-km) route by the aircraft on a more or less regular basis since December 26, 1975. The Moscow—Alma Ata service was suspended in June 1978, following the loss of a Tu-144 while undergoing tests, and the airliner had not been returned to service by the beginning of 1979, although Aeroflot stated that the return of the Tu-144 to regular service was "imminent". However, it is reported that problems of excessive cabin noise and vibration, and poor cruise efficiency, remain unresolved.

TUPOLEV TU-144 (CHARGER)

Dimensions: Span, 91 ft $10\frac{1}{3}$ in (28,00 m); length, 211 ft $5\frac{1}{8}$ in (64,45 m); height, 142 ft 3 in (12,85 m); wing area, 4,714·6 sq ft (438 m²).

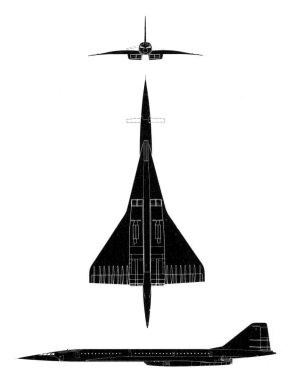

TUPOLEV TU-154B (CARELESS)

Country of Origin: USSR.
Type: Medium- to long-haul commercial transport.
Power Plant: Three 23,150 lb (10 500 kg) Kuznetsov NK-8-2U turbofans.
Performance: Max. cruise, 590 mph (950 km/h) at 31,000 ft (9 450 m); econ. cruise, 559 mph (900 km/h) at 36,090 ft (11 000 m); range (with max. payload—39,683 lb), 1,710 mls (2 750 km), (with 160 passengers), 2,020 mls (3 250 km), (with 120 passengers), 2,485 mls (4 000 km).
Weights: Max. take-off, 211,644 lb (96 000 kg).
Accommodation: Crew of three on flight-deck and basic arrangements for 160 single-class passengers in six-abreast seating, eight first-class and 150 tourist-class passengers, or (high density) 169 passengers.
Status: Prototype Tu-154 flown on October 4, 1968, current production model being the Tu-154B (introduced by Aeroflot in 1976) of which approximately four per month were being manufactured at the beginning of 1979. More than 300 Tu-154s (all versions) are currently in service with Aeroflot and the Tu-154B has also been supplied to Malev (three) of Hungary.
Notes: The Tu-154B combines the improvements introduced by the Tu-154A with major changes in controls and systems, and slight increases in weights. The wing spoilers have been extended in span and are now used for low-speed lateral control and passenger capacity has been increased by extending the usable cabin area rearwards, and an extra emergency exit has been added in each side of the fuselage. Various longer-range versions of the basic Tu-154 are known to be under study, including one reportedly powered by NK-86 turbofans similar to those of the Il-86.

TUPOLEV TU-154B (CARELESS)

Dimensions: Span, 123 ft 2½ in (37,55 m); length, 157 ft 1¾ in (47,90 m); height, 37 ft 4¾ in (11,40 m); wing area, 2,168·92 sq ft (201,45 m²).

TUPOLEV TU-26 (BACKFIRE-B)

Country of Origin: USSR.

Type: Long-range strike and maritime reconnaissance-strike aircraft.

Power Plant: Two (estimated) 33,070 lb (15 000 kg) dry and 46,300 lb (21 000 kg) reheat Kuznetsov turbofans.

Performance: (Estimated) Max. (short-period) speed, 1,320 mph (2 125 km/h) at 39,370 ft (12 000 m) or Mach 2·0; max. sustained speed, 1,190 mph (1 915 km/h) at 39,370 ft (12 000 m) or Mach 1·8, 685 mph (1 100 km/h) at sea level or Mach 0·9; cruise, 495 mph (795 km/h) at sea level or Mach 0·65, 530 mph (850 km/h) at 39,370 ft (12 000 m) or Mach 0·8; unrefuelled combat radius (including 400 mls/250 km at Mach 1·8), 2,485 mls (4 000 km) for HI-LO-HI (200 mls/320 km at low altitude) profile.

Weights: (Estimated) Operational empty, 114,640 lb (52 000 kg); max. take-off, 260,000 lb (118 000 kg).

Armament: One or two externally-mounted AS-6 Kingfish 340-mile (740-km) range inertially-guided stand-off missiles or internal weapons load of approx. 15,000 lb (6 800 kg). Remotely-controlled 23-mm cannon tail barbette.

Status: Reported in prototype form in 1969, the Backfire apparently began to enter service with both the Soviet long-range aviation and the Naval Air Force in 1974, with combined total of 120–130 in service at beginning of 1979, when production was reported to be 30–40 annually.

TUPOLEV TU-26 (BACKFIRE-B)

Dimensions: (Estimated) Span (max.), 115 ft 0 in (35,00 m), (min.), 92 ft 0 in (28,00 m); length, 138 ft 0 in (42,00 m); height, 29 ft 6 in (9,00 m); wing area, 1,830 sq ft (170 m²).

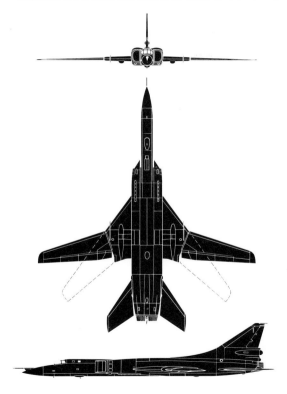

VALMET VINKA

Country of Origin: Finland.

Type: Side-by-side two-seat primary trainer.

Power Plant: One 200 hp Avco Lycoming IO-360-A1B6 four-cylinder horizontally-opposed engine.

Performance: (At 2,204 lb/1 000 kg) Max. speed, 149 mph (240 km/h) at sea level; econ. cruise (75% power), 138 mph (222 km/h) at 5,000 ft (1 525 m); range (with max. fuel), 630 mls (1 015 km); initial climb, 1,120 ft/min (5,69 m/sec); service ceiling, 16,400 ft (5 000 m).

Weights: Operational empty, 1,631 lb (740 kg); max. take-off (aerobatic), 2,204 lb (1 000 kg), (normal), 2,645 lb (1 200 kg).

Status: Prototype flown July 1, 1975, and production deliveries scheduled to commence early 1979 against Finnish Air Force order for 30 aircraft placed in November 1976. Two additional aircraft laid down for development and demonstration purposes.

Notes: The Vinka (Blast) was designed to meet the requirements of a specification drawn up by the Finnish Air Force and its cockpit provides space for an additional pair of seats or up to 661 lb (330 kg) of freight. The Vinka may also be adapted for the aeromedical role (with a single casualty stretcher and a medical attendant in addition to the pilot), for aerial photography and for glider towing, and the wheel undercarriage may be replaced by skis.

VALMET VINKA

Dimensions: Span, 30 ft 6¼ in (9,30 m); length, 23 ft 11½ in (7,30 m); wing area, 150·69 sq ft (14,00 m²).

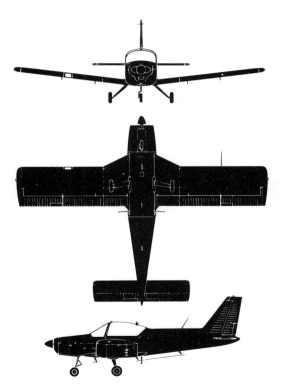

VOUGHT TA-7C CORSAIR II

Country of Origin: USA.

Type: Tandem two-seat combat crew trainer.

Power Plant: One 13,400 lb (6 078 kg) Pratt & Whitney TF30-P-408 turbofan.

Performance: Max. speed, 679 mph (1 093 km/h) at sea level; tactical radius, 792 mls (1 275 km); ferry range (without external stores), 2,268 mls (3 650 km).

Weights: Empty, 19,180 lb (8 700 kg); max. take-off (without external stores), 30,828 lb (13 984 kg).

Armament: One 20-mm M-61A-1 rotary cannon with 1,000 rounds and ordnance loads of up to 15,000 lb (6 804 kg) on six wing and two fuselage stations.

Status: The first two-seat Corsair II (the YA-7E converted from the first TF41-powered A-7E) was flown on August 29, 1972, and 60 similar conversions (of earlier TF30-powered A-7Bs and A-7Cs) have been ordered by the US Navy as TA-7Cs, deliveries having commenced in October 1978, and conversions continuing at beginning of 1979. An unspecified (as at beginning of 1979) number of Air National Guard A-7Ds are to be converted in similar fashion to TA-7Ds and the Hellenic Air Force is to receive six (one conversion and five new-built) TA-7Hs during 1980.

Notes: The TA-7 is a derivative of the single-seat A-7 with a 34-in (86,4-cm) fuselage plug to accommodate a second cockpit and marginally larger vertical tail surfaces. The TA-7C is a shipboard trainer, but the TA-7D and TA-7H will be powered by the 15,000 lb (6 804 kg) Allison TF41-A-2 (Spey) turbofan, will have the jet fuel on-board starter of the equivalent single-seat models (see 1978 edition) and will not have aerial refuelling capability.

VOUGHT TA-7C CORSAIR II

Dimensions: Span, 38 ft 8¾ in (11,80 m); length, 48 ft 8 in (14,80 m); height, 16 ft 3⅝ in (4,97 m); wing area, 375 sq ft (34,83 m²).

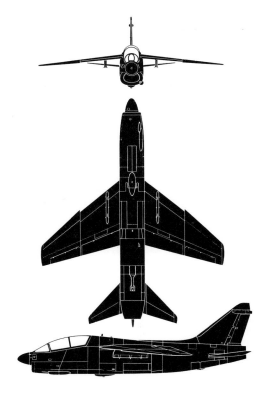

YAKOVLEV YAK-36MP (FORGER-A)

Country of Origin: USSR.

Type: Single-seat shipboard air defence and strike fighter.

Power Plant: One (approx.) 17,640 lb (8 000 kg) lift/cruise turbojet plus two 7,935 lb (3 600 kg) lift turbojets.

Performance: (Estimated) Max. speed, 695 mph (1 120 km/h) above 36,000 ft (10 970 m), or Mach 1·05, 725 mph (1 167 km/h) at sea level, or Mach 0·95; high-speed cruise, 595 mph (958 km/h) at 20,000 ft (6 095 m), or Mach 0·85; combat radius (internal fuel and 2,205-lb/1 000-kg external ordnance), 230 mls (370 km), (with two 110 Imp gal/500 l drop tanks, a reconnaissance pod and two AAMs), 340 mls (547 km); initial climb, 20,000 ft/min (101,6 m/sec).

Weights: (Estimated) Empty, 12,125 lb (5 500 kg); max. take-off, 22,000 lb (9 980 kg).

Armament: Four underwing pylons with total capacity of (approx.) 2,205 lb (1 000 kg), including twin-barrel 23-mm cannon pods, air-to-air missiles or bombs.

Status: The Yak-36MP (Forger-A) is believed to have flown in prototype form in 1971 and to have attained service evaluation status in 1976 aboard the carrier *Kiev*.

Notes: Possessing no short-landing-and-take-off (STOL) capability, being limited to vertical-take-off-and-landing (VTOL operation), the Yak-36 combines a vectored-thrust lift/cruise engine with fore and aft lift engines. The single-seat Yak-36MP possesses no attack radar and no internal armament. A tandem two-seat version, the Yak-36UV (Forger-B), has an extended forward fuselage. A second seat is added ahead of that of the Yak-36MP and the nose is drooped to provide a measure of vertical stagger and the aft fuselage is also extended in order to maintain the CG. The two-seat conversion training version is illustrated above.

YAKOVLEV YAK-36MP (FORGER-A)

Dimensions: (Estimated) Span, 24 ft 7 in (7,50 m); length,
52 ft 6 in (16,00 m); height, 11 ft 0 in (3,35 m); wing area,
167 sq ft (15,50 m²).

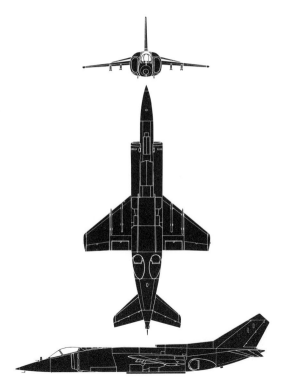

YAKOVLEV YAK-42 (CLOBBER)

Country of Origin: USSR.

Type: Short- to medium-haul commercial transport.

Power Plant: Three 14,320 lb (6 500 kg) Lotarev D-36 turbofans.

Performance: Econ. cruise, 510 mph (820 km/h) at 25,000 ft (7 600 m): range (max. payload—31,938 lb/14 500 kg), 620 mls (1 000 km), (with 26,430-lb/12 000-kg payload), 1,150 mls (1 850 km); max. range, 1,520 mls (2 450 km); time to cruise altitude (25,000 ft/7 600 m), 11 min.

Weights: Operational empty, 63,845 lb (28 960 kg); max. take-off, 114,640 lb (52 000 kg).

Accommodation: Basic flight crew of two and various alternative cabin arrangements, including 76 passengers in a mixed-class layout (16 first class), 100 passengers in a single-class layout with six-abreast seating and 120 passengers in a high-density layout.

Status: First prototype flown on March 7, 1975, followed by second in April 1976. A production prototype was flown in February 1977, and deliveries to Aeroflot are scheduled to commence during the first quarter of 1979.

Notes: The initial prototypes of the Yak-42 differed one from the other in wing sweep angle, the first prototype featuring 11 deg of sweepback and the second 25 deg, the latter sweep angle being adopted for production aircraft. The Yak-42 is intended for operation primarily over relatively short stages and utilising restricted airfields with poor surfaces and limited facilities in the remoter areas of the Soviet Union. Independent of airport ground equipment and having a heavy-duty undercarriage, the Yak-42 bears a close resemblance to the smaller Yak-40 (see 1977 edition).

YAKOVLEV YAK-42 (CLOBBER)

Dimensions: Span, 112 ft 2½ in (34,20 m); length, 119 ft 4 in (36,38 m); height, 32 ft 3 in (9,83 m); wing area, 1,615 sq ft (150,00 m²).

YAKOVLEV YAK-52

Country of Origin: USSR.
Type: Tandem two-seat primary trainer.
Power Plant: One 360 hp Ivchenko M-14P nine-cylinder radial air-cooled engine.
Performance: Max. speed, 177 mph (285 km/h); range, 329 mls (530 km); endurance, 2·85 hrs; initial climb, 1,970 ft/min (10 m/sec); service ceiling, 19,700 ft (6 000 m).
Weights: Empty, 2,202 lb (1 000 kg); max. take-off, 2,840 lb (1 290 kg).
Status: Prototype flown in 1976, and series production scheduled to commence during 1979 for the DOSAAF aero clubs. Manufacture to be undertaken in Romania.
Notes: Derived from the aerobatic single-seat Yak-50 competition aircraft (see 1977 edition), the Yak-52 is intended as a successor to the ubiquitous Yak-18 as the standard primary trainer of Soviet flying schools and, although intended for *ab initio* training, it is fully aerobatic and possesses a high power-to-weight ratio—7·3 lb/hp (3,3 kg/cv)—in aerobatic configuration. Apart from the tandem two-seat cockpit, the Yak-52 differs from the Yak-50 primarily in undercarriage arrangement, the tail-down undercarriage of the single-seater having been replaced by a tricycle, the main legs of which retract forwards leaving the wheels fully exposed. Under Comecon arrangements, the main production of the Yak-52 for Soviet schools will be undertaken by the Romanian aircraft industry.

YAKOVLEV YAK-52

Dimensions: Span, 31 ft 2 in (9,50 m); length, 25 ft 2 in (7,68 m); wing area, 161·5 sq ft (15,00 m²).

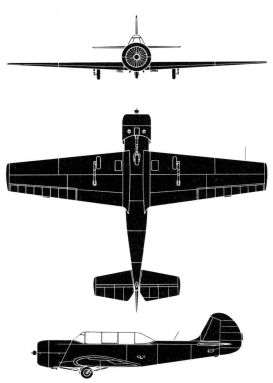

AÉROSPATIALE SA 319B ALOUETTE III

Country of Origin: France.
Type: Light utility helicopter (seven seats).
Power Plant: One 789 shp Turboméca Astazou XIVH turbo-shaft.
Performance: Max. speed, 137 mph (220 km/h) at sea level; max. cruise, 122 mph (197 km/h); max. inclined climb, 885 ft/min (4,49 m/sec); hovering ceiling (in ground effect), 10,170 ft (3 100 m), (out of ground effect), 5,575 ft (1 700 m); range (six passengers), 375 mls (605 km).
Weights: Empty, 2,442 lb (1 108 kg); max. take-off, 4,960 lb (2 250 kg).
Dimensions: Rotor diam, 36 ft 1¾ in (11,02 m); fuselage length, 32 ft 10¾ in (10,03 m).
Notes: The SA 319B is an Astazou-powered derivative of the Artouste-powered SA 316B Alouette III. All Alouette IIIs built prior to 1970 had the Artouste turboshaft, and approximately 1,400 Alouette IIIs (all versions) had been ordered by 72 countries by the beginning of 1979. Licence production has been undertaken in India, Romania and Switzerland. The naval version fulfils a variety of shipborne roles and for the ASW task may be fitted with search radar, MAD (Magnet Anomaly Detection) equipment and two Mk 44 homing torpedoes. The SA 319B may also be fitted with a gyro-stabilised sight and two wire-guided AS.12 or four AS.11 missiles for the anti-armour role.

AÉROSPATIALE SA 330J PUMA

Country of Origin: France.

Type: Medium transport helicopter.

Power Plant: Two 1,575 shp Turboméca IVC turboshafts.

Performance: Max. speed, 163 mph (262 km/h); max. continuous cruise at sea level, 159 mph (257 km/h); max. inclined climb, 1,400 ft/min (7,1 m/sec); hovering ceiling (in ground effect), 7,315 ft (2 230 m), (out of ground effect), 4,430 ft (1 350 m); max. range (standard fuel), 342 mls (550 km).

Weights: Operational empty, 10,060 lb (4 563 kg); max. take-off, 16,315 lb (7 400 kg).

Dimensions: Rotor diam, 49 ft 2½ in (15,00 m); fuselage length, 46 ft 1½ in (14,06 m).

Notes: The civil SA 330J and the equivalent military SA 330L (illustrated) were the current production models of the Puma at the beginning of 1979 when more than 600 Pumas of all versions had been ordered. The SA 330J and 330L differ from the civil SA 330F (passenger) and SA 330G (cargo), and SA 330H (military) models that immediately preceded them in having new plastic blades accompanied by increases in gross weights. The SA 330B (French Army), SA 330C (export) and SA 330E (RAF) had 1,328 shp Turmo IIIC4 turboshafts. Components for the Puma are supplied by Westland in the UK (representing approx. 15% of the airframe) and production was 8–10 Pumas monthly at the beginning of 1979. The Puma has been delivered to some 40 countries.

AÉROSPATIALE SA 332 SUPER PUMA

Country of Origin: France.
Type: Medium transport helicopter (21 seats).
Power Plant: Two 1,700 shp Turboméca Makila I turbo-shafts.
Performance: Max. cruising speed, 178 mph (287 km/h); hovering ceiling (out of ground effect), 9.514 ft (2 900 m); range (with standard reserve), 400 mls (645 km); endurance, 3·5 hrs.
Weights: Empty, 8,344 lb (3 785 kg); max. take-off, 16,755 lb (7 600 kg).
Dimensions: Similar to SA 330 Puma.
Notes: The SA 332 Super Puma, the first production-standard prototype of which commenced its test programme on September 13, 1978, is the definitive version of the upgraded SA 330 Puma, the main differences being the twin-Makila power plant with uprated and simplified transmission, composite rotor blades, new avionics and larger-capacity fuselage. The military version of the Super Puma will accommodate 21 fully-equipped troops, or six casualty stretchers and seven seated wounded/medical attendants, and anti-submarine warfare and commercial models are envisaged, initial deliveries of both military and civil variants commencing in the second half of 1980. Production of the Super Puma will be shared by Westland Helicopters in the UK. The Makila-powered SA 331 test-bed first flew on September 5, 1977.

AÉROSPATIALE SA 342 GAZELLE

Country of Origin: France.

Type: Five-seat light utility helicopter.

Power Plant: One 870 shp Turboméca Astazou XIVH turbo-shaft.

Performance: Max. speed, 193 mph (310 km/h); max. continuous cruise at sea level, 168 mph (270 km/h); max. inclined climb, 2,066 ft/min (10,5 m/sec); hovering ceiling (in ground effect), 13,120 ft (4 000 m), (out of ground effect), 10,330 ft (3 150 m); range at sea level, 488 mls (785 km).

Weights: Empty equipped, 2,114 lb (959 kg); max. take-off, 4,190 lb (1 900 kg).

Dimensions: Rotor diam, 34 ft 5½ in (10,50 m); fuselage length, 31 ft 2¾ in (9,53 m).

Notes: The SA 342 is a more powerful derivative of the SA 341 (592 shp Astazou IIIA) and has been exported to Kuwait, Iraq and elsewhere, and is equipped to launch four HOT missiles, AS-11s or other weapons. A civil equivalent, the SA 342J offering a 220 lb (100 kg) increase in payload, became available in 1977, and sales of the SA 341 and 342 Gazelles exceeded 770 by the beginning of 1979. Versions of the lower-powered SA 341 comprise the SA 341B (British Army), SA 341C (British Navy), SA 341D (RAF), SA 341F (French Army), SA 341G (civil version) and SA 341H (military export version). Sub-assemblies are supplied by Westland, final assembly being by Aérospatiale.

AÉROSPATIALE AS 350 ECUREUIL

Country of Origin: France.
Type: Light general-purpose utility helicopter.
Power Plant: One 740 shp Turboméca Arriel or 592 shp Avco Lycoming LTS 101 turboshaft.
Performance: (Arriel turboshaft) Max. speed, 166 mph (267 km/h); max. continuous cruise at sea level, 143 mph (230 km/h); hovering ceiling (in ground effect), 10,660 ft (3 250 m), (out of ground effect), 8,200 ft (2 500 m); range, 430 mls (690 km).
Weights: Empty equipped, 2,094 lb (950 kg); max. take-off, 4,630 lb (2 100 kg).
Dimensions: Rotor diam, 35 ft 0¾ in (10,69 m); fuselage length, 35 ft 9½ in (10,91 m).
Notes: First (LTS 101-powered) Ecureuil (Squirrel) prototype flown on June 27, 1974, with second (Arriel-powered) following in February 1975. The Ecureuil is being offered with both the above-mentioned turboshafts and the first two of eight pre-series examples (both LTS 101 and Arriel-powered) were completed late in 1976 with the first customer deliveries effected in the first half of 1978. The standard production model is a six-seater and features include a Starflex all-plastic rotor head, simplified dynamic machinery and modular assemblies to simplify changes in the field. The Ecureuil is known in the USA as the AS 350D AStar. Orders for some 450 by beginning of 1979, when output was building up to 20 monthly.

AÉROSPATIALE SA 361 DAUPHIN

Country of Origin: France.
Type: Multi-purpose and transport helicopter.
Power Plant: One 1,282 shp Turboméca Astazou XX turbo-shaft.
Performance: Max. speed, 196 mph (315 km/h) at sea level; cruise, 175 mph (282 km/h) at sea level; max. inclined climb rate, 1,969 ft/min (10 m/sec); hovering ceiling (in ground effect), 13,450 ft (4 100 m), (out of ground effect), 10,990 ft (3 350 m); range, 425 mls (685 km).
Weights: Empty equipped, 3,487 lb (1 582 kg); max. take-off, 6,800 lb (3 300 kg).
Dimensions. Rotor diam, 38 ft 4 in (11,68 m); fuselage length, 36 ft 0½ (10,98 m).
Notes: The SA 361 is an overpowered version of the SA 360 (see 1977 edition) intended specifically for hot-and-high operating conditions. The military version, the SA 361H, can carry up to eight HOT (High-subsonic Optically-guided Tube-launched) anti-armour missiles, and deliveries of this helicopter (and its civil equivalent, the SA 361F) commenced in the second half of 1978. Like the lower-powered SA 360, the SA 361 will accommodate up to 10 persons, and the slung load may be increased by 440 lb (200 kg) to 3,304 lb (1 500 kg). The first prototype Dauphin flew on June 2, 1972, and some 75 Dauphin family helicopters ordered by 1979, and the proto-type of the SA 361 version flew on July 12, 1976.

AÉROSPATIALE SA 365 DAUPHIN 2

Country of Origin: France.

Type: Multi-purpose and transport helicopter.

Power Plant: Two 680 shp Turboméca Arriel turboshafts.

Performance: Max. speed, 196 mph (315 km/h); max. continuous cruise at sea level, 163 mph (262 km/h); max. inclined climb rate, 1,653 ft/min (8,4 m/s); hovering ceiling (both in and out of ground effect), 15,000 ft (4 575 m); range, 339 mls (545 km).

Weights: Empty equipped, 3,980 lb (1 806 kg); max. take-off, 7,495 lb (3 400 kg).

Dimensions: Main rotor diam, 37 ft 8¾ in (11,50 m); fuselage length, 36 ft 3⅞ in (10,98 m).

Notes: First flown on January 24, 1975, with production deliveries commencing early in 1978, the SA 365 Dauphin 2 can accommodate up to 14 persons. Fitted with an all-plastic Starflex rotor head, the Dauphin 2 is offered for both civil and military roles, a proposed naval version (SA 365N) having a retractable nosewheel undercarriage, stepped cockpit, nose-mounted search radar, a gyro-stabilised weapons aiming sight, MAD (Magnetic Anomaly Detection) equipment, radio-command AS-15 anti-shipping missiles, and folding main rotor blades and vertical fin. The SA 365N has Arriel 2 turboshaft uprated to 735 shp. A variant of the Dauphine 2, the SA 366 powered by two Avco Lycoming LTS101 turboshafts, was tested in prototype form but subsequently shelved.

224

AGUSTA A 109A

Country of Origin: Italy.
Type: Eight-seat light utility helicopter.
Power Plant: Two 420 shp Allison 250-C20B turboshafts.
Performance: (At 5,402 lb/2 450 kg) Max. speed, 192 mph (310 km/h); max. continuous cruise, 173 mph (278 km/h) at sea level; hovering ceiling (in ground effect), 9,800 ft (2 987 m), (out of ground effect), 6,700 ft (2 042 m); max. inclined climb, 1,600 ft/min (8,12 m/sec); max. range, 385 mls (620 km) at 148 mph (238 km/h).
Weights: Empty equipped, 2,998 lb (1 360 kg); max. take-off, 5,402 lb (2 450 kg).
Dimensions: Rotor diam, 36 ft 1 in (11,00 m); fuselage length, 36 ft 10$\frac{7}{8}$ in (11,25 m).
Notes: The first of four A 109A prototypes flew on August 4, 1971. A pre-production batch of 10 A 109As was followed by first customer deliveries late 1976 with nearly 100 delivered by beginning of 1979, when production was rising from six to 10–12 monthly. The A 109A is currently being offered for both civil and military roles, five having been delivered to the Italian Army, including two equipped to launch TOW (Tube-launched Optically-tracked Wire-guided) missiles, one of these being illustrated above. Proposed variants include a naval A 109A with search radar, gyro-stabilised weapons aiming sight and torpedo or rocket armament, and the A 129 light anti-armour helicopter utilising some of the dynamic components.

AGUSTA-BELL AB 212ASW

Country of Origin: Italy.
Type: Anti-submarine and anti-surface vessel helicopter.
Power Plant: One 1,290 shp (derated from 1,875 shp) Pratt & Whitney PT6T-6 coupled turboshaft.
Performance: (At 11,197 lb/5 080 kg) Max. speed, 122 mph (196 km/h) at sea level; max. cruise, 115 mph (185 km/h); max. inclined climb, 1,450 ft/min (7,38 m/sec); hovering ceiling (in ground effect), 12,500 ft (3 810 m), (out of ground effect), 4,000 ft (1,220 m); range (15% reserves), 414 mls (667 km) at sea level.
Weights: Empty equipped, 7,540 lb (3 420 kg); max. take-off, 11,197 lb (5 080 kg).
Dimensions: Rotor diam, 48 ft 2½ in (14,69 m); fuselage length, 42 ft 10¾ in (13,07 m).
Notes: The AB 212ASW is an Italian anti-submarine derivative of the Bell 212 Twin Two-Twelve (see page 230) developed primarily for use by the Italian Navy (to which 28 examples are being delivered) and for export (batches having been delivered to Peru, Spain and Turkey). For the ASW mission, the AB 212ASW carries high-performance long-range search radar, ECM equipment, a gyro-stabilised sighting system and a pair of Mk 44 or Mk 46 homing torpedoes or depth charges. Agusta also manufactures the standard AB 212 and the AB 205 Iroquois, combined production rate being 12–15 monthly at the beginning of 1979.

BELL MODEL 206B JETRANGER III

Country of Origin: USA.
Type: Five-seat light utility helicopter.
Power Plant: One 420 shp Allison 250-C20B turboshaft.
Performance: (At 3,200 lb/1 451 kg) Max. speed, 140 mph (225 km/h) at sea level; max. cruise, 133 mph (214 km/h) at sea level; hovering ceiling (in ground effect), 12,700 ft (3 871 m), (out of ground effect), 6,000 ft (1 829 m); max. range (no reserve), 360 mls (579 km).
Weights: Empty, 1,500 lb (680 kg); max. take-off, 3,200 lb (1 451 kg).
Dimensions: Rotor diam, 33 ft 4 in (10,16 m); fuselage length, 31 ft 2 in (9,50 m).
Notes: Introduced in 1977, with deliveries commencing in July of that year, the JetRanger III differs from the JetRanger II which it supplants in having an uprated engine, an enlarged and improved tail rotor mast and more minor changes. Some 2,700 commercial JetRangers had been delivered by the beginning of 1979, both commercial and military versions (including production by licensees) totalling more than 6,000. A light observation version of the JetRanger for the US Army is designated OH-58 Kiowa and a training version for the US Navy is known as the TH-57A SeaRanger. The JetRanger is built by Agusta in Italy as the AB 206, and the JetRanger II has been built in Australia. A retrofit kit is available to bring earlier JetRangers to Srs.III standard.

BELL MODEL 206L LONGRANGER

Country of Origin: USA.
Type: Seven-seat light utility helicopter.
Power Plant: One 420 shp Allison 250-C20B turboshaft.
Performance: (At 3,900 lb/1 769 kg) Max. speed, 144 mph
(232 km/h); cruise, 136 mph (229 km/h) at sea level;
hovering ceiling (in ground effect), 8,200 ft (2 499 m), (out
of ground effect), 2,000 ft (610 m); range, 390 mls (628 km)
at sea level, 430 mls (692 km) at 5,000 ft (1 524 m).
Weights: Empty, 1,861 lb (844 kg); max. take-off, 4,000 lb
(1 814 kg).
Dimensions: Rotor diam. 37 ft 0 in (11,28 m); fuselage
length, 33 ft 3 in (10,13 m).
Notes: The Model 206L LongRanger is a stretched and more
powerful version of the Model 206B JetRanger III, with a long
fuselage, increased fuel capacity, an uprated engine and a
larger rotor. The LongRanger is being manufactured in parallel
with the JetRanger III and initial customer deliveries commenced in October 1975, prototype testing having been initiated on September 11, 1974. The LongRanger is available with
emergency flotation gear and with a 2,000-lb (907-kg)
capacity cargo hook. In the aeromedical or rescue role the
LongRanger can accommodate two casualty stretches and
two ambulatory casualties. The 206L-1 LongRanger II has a
500 shp 250-C28B engine. Production was 15 monthly at the
beginning of 1979.

228

BELL MODEL 209 HUEYCOBRA

Country of Origin: USA.

Type: Two-seat attack helicopter.

Power Plant: One (AH-1J) 1,800 shp Pratt & Whitney (Canada) T400-CP-400 or (AH-1T) 1,970 shp T400-WV-402 coupled turboshaft.

Performance: (AH-1J at 10,000 lb/4 535 kg) Max. speed, 207 mph (333 km/h) at sea level; max. inclined climb, 1,090 ft/min (5,54 m/sec); hovering ceiling (in ground effect), 12,450 ft (3 794 m); max. range (without reserves), 359 mls (577 km).

Weights: Empty equipped (AH-1J), 6,816 lb (3 091 kg), (AH-1T) 8,489 lb (3 854 kg); max. take-off (AH-1J), 10,000 lb (4 535 kg), (AH-1T), 14,000 lb (6 356 kg).

Dimensions: Rotor diam (AH-1J), 44 ft 0 in (13,41 m), (AH-1T) 48 ft 0 in (14,64 m); fuselage length (AH-1J), 44 ft 7 in (13,59 m), (AH-1T) 45 ft 3 in (13,79 m).

Notes: The twin-engined (coupled turboshaft) version of the Model 209 is being produced in two versions, the first of these, the AH-1J, being essentially a "Twin Pac" powered version of the US Marine Corps' AH-1G SeaCobra (1,100 shp Lycoming T53-L-13), and in addition to being supplied to the USMC, this model is being manufactured for Iran (202 examples). The AH-1T (illustrated) flew in 1976 and differs in having the dynamic components of the Model 214 (see page 231), and delivery of 57 on order for the USMC commenced late in 1977.

BELL MODEL 212 TWIN TWO-TWELVE

Country of Origin: USA.
Type: Fifteen-seat utility helicopter.
Power Plant: One 1,800 shp Pratt & Whitney PT6T-3 coupled turboshaft.
Performance: Max. speed, 121 mph (194 km/h) at sea level; max. inclined climb at 10,000 lb (4 535 kg), 1,460 ft/min (7,4 m/sec); hovering ceiling (in ground effect), 17,100 ft (5 212 m), (out of ground effect), 9,900 ft (3 020 m); max. range, 296 mls (476 km) at sea level.
Weights: Empty, 5,500 lb (2 495 kg); max. take-off, 10,000 lb (4 535 kg).
Dimensions: Rotor diam, 48 ft 2½ in (14,69 m); fuselage length, 42 ft 10¾ in (13,07 m).
Notes: The Model 212 is based on the Model 205 (see 1977 Edition) from which it differs primarily in having a twin-engined power plant (two turboshaft engines coupled to a combining gearbox with a single output shaft), and both commercial and military versions are being produced. A model for the Canadian Armed Forces is designated CUH-1N, and an essentially similar variant of the Model 212, the UH-1N, is being supplied to the USAF, the USN and the USMC. All versions of the Model 212 can carry an external load of 4,400 lb (1 814 kg), and can maintain cruise performance on one engine component at maximum gross weight.

BELL MODEL 214ST

Country of Origin: USA.
Type: Medium transport helicopter (19 seats).
Power Plant: Two 1,625 shp (limited to combined output of 2,250 shp) General Electric T700-T1C (CT7-2) turboshafts.
Performance: Max. cruising speed, 173 mph (278 km/h); econ. cruise, 155–167 mph (249–269 km/h); hovering ceiling (out of ground effect), 6,000 ft (1 830 m); range (with 20 min reserve), 460 mls (740 km).
Weights: Max. take-off, 16,500 lb (7 491 kg).
Dimensions: Rotor diam, 52 ft 0 in (15,85 m); fuselage length, 50 ft 1 in (15,26 m).
Notes: The Model 214ST is a significantly improved derivative of the Model 214B BigLifter (see 1978 edition), and both military and commercial models are planned, and some of the 350 examples of the former ordered by the Iranian Government were originally to have been assembled in Iran under a co-production programme cancelled in December 1978. The Model 214ST test-bed was first flown in March 1977, and three representative prototypes (one in military configuration and two for commercial certification) are scheduled to commence their test programme during the first half of 1979, production deliveries commencing in 1980. As a high-density military transport, the Model 214ST will accommodate 17 troops and a tactical combat version will carry a crew of four and a 12-man squad, while the commercial model will accommodate 16 passengers.

BELL MODEL 222

Country of Origin: USA.

Type: Light utility and transport helicopter.

Power Plant: Two 650 shp Avco Lycoming LTS 101-650C turboshafts.

Performance: Max. cruise, 165 mph (266 km/h) at sea level; range cruise, 150 mph (241 km/h) at sea level; hovering ceiling (in ground effect), 10,300 ft (3 140 m), (out of ground effect), 6,400 ft (1950 m); range (20 min reserve), 450 mls (724 km) at 8,000 ft (2 438 m).

Weights: Empty, 4,250 lb (1 928 kg); normal take-off, 7,200 lb (3 266 kg).

Dimensions: Rotor diam, 30 ft 0 in (11,89 m); fuselage length, 39 ft 9 in (12,12 m).

Notes: Designed to accommodate up to 10 persons (including pilot) in a high-density arrangement, with a standard interior providing eight seats and an executive six-seat layout, the Model 222 is the first US light twin-turbine helicopter and the first of five prototypes was flown on August 13, 1976, with production deliveries scheduled for October 1979. The Model 222 may be fitted with flotation gear of fixed skids as alternatives to the retractable tricycle wheel undercarriage, and kits will be available to adapt it for use in the aeromedical role, with accommodation for two casualty stretchers and two perambulatory casualties or medical attendants. A total of 137 is scheduled to be delivered by the end of 1980, and production will attain 15 monthly in 1981.

BOEING VERTOL MODEL 114

Country of Origin: USA.
Type: Medium transport helicopter.
Power Plant: (CH-47C) Two 3,750 shp Lycoming T55-L-11 turboshafts.
Performance: (CH-47C at 33,000 lb/14 969 kg) Max. speed, 190 mph (306 km/h) at sea level; average cruise, 158 mph (254 km/h); max. inclined climb, 2,880 ft/min (14,63 m/sec); hovering ceiling (out of ground effect), 14,750 ft (4 495 m); mission radius, 115 mls (185 km).
Weights: Empty, 20,378 lb (9 243); max. take-off, 46,000 lb (20 865 kg).
Dimensions: Rotor diam (each), 60 ft 0 in (18,29 m); fuselage length, 51 ft 0 in (15,54 m).
Notes: The Model 114 is the standard medium transport helicopter of the US Army, and is operated by that service under the designation CH-47 Chinook. The initial production model, the CH-47A, was powered by 2,200 shp T55-L-5 or 2,650 shp T55-L-7 turboshafts. This was succeeded by the CH-47B with 2,850 shp T55-L-7C engines, redesigned rotor blades and other modifications, and this, in turn, gave place to the current CH-47C with more powerful engines, strengthened transmissions, and increased fuel capacity. This model is manufactured in Italy by Elicotteri Meriodionali, orders calling for 24 (of 26) for the Italian Army, 20 for Libya and 57 (of 95) for the Iranian Army.

ENSTROM 280L HAWK

Country of Origin: USA.
Type: Four-seat light utility helicopter.
Power Plant: One 225 hp Avco Lycoming HIO-360-G1AD four-cylinder horizontally-opposed engine.
Performance: Max. speed, 117 mph (188 km/h); cruise, 106 mph (170 km/h); max. inclined climb, 1,000 ft/min (5,1 m/sec); hovering ceiling (in ground effect), 8,000 ft (2 438 m); range (no reserves), 203 mls.
Weights: Empty, 1,562 lb (709 kg); max. take-off, 2,600 lb (1 250 kg).
Dimensions: Rotor diam, 34 ft 0 in (10,36 m); length (overall), 32 ft 4 in (9,84 m).
Notes: The Model 280L Hawk is the latest variant in the range of Enstrom light helicopters, some 600 examples of which had been delivered in the period up to the beginning of 1979. The Hawk joins in production the F-28C and Model 280C, both powered by a turbo-supercharged Avco Lycoming HIO-360-E1AD, the F-28F Falcon and the related Model 280F, both having the more powerful HIO-360-G1AD engine, similar to that of the Hawk, and an enlarged forward fuselage, and a combined production rate of 15 helicopters monthly is anticipated by the end of 1979, when deliveries of the fully-certificated Hawk are scheduled to commence. The Hawk airframe is to be adapted for the Allison 250–20B turboshaft as the Eagle.

HUGHES 500M-D TOW DEFENDER

Country of Origin: USA.

Type: Light anti-armour helicopter.

Power Plant: One 420 shp Allison 250-C20B turboshaft.

Performance: (At 3,000 lb/1 362 kg) Max. speed, 175 mph (282 km/h) at sea level; cruise, 160 mph (257 km/h) at 4,000 ft (1 220 m); max. inclined climb, 1,920 ft/min (9,75 m/sec); hovering ceiling (in ground effect), 8,800 ft (2 682 m), (out of ground effect), 7,100 ft (2 164 m); max. range, 263 mls (423 km).

Weights: Empty, 1,295 lb (588 kg); max. take-off (internal load), 3,000 lb (1 362 kg), (with external load), 3,620 lb (1 642 kg).

Dimensions: Rotor diam, 26 ft 5 in (8,05 m); fuselage length, 21 ft 5 in (6,52 m).

Notes: The Model 500M-D is a multi-role military helicopter derived, via the civil Model 500D, from the US Army's OH-6A Cayuse observation helicopter. The TOW Defender version is an anti-armour helicopter with 7,62-mm armour for the crew, engine compressor and fuel control, and provision for four TOW (Tube-launched Optically-tracked Wire-guided) missiles. Various alternative weapons may be fitted, including seven-round launchers for 2·75-in rockets, a 30-mm chain gun on the fuselage side or a 7,62-mm chain gun in an extendible ventral turret. The Defender is being manufactured in South Korea under a co-production arrangement.

235

HUGHES AH-64

Country of Origin: USA.

Type: Tandem two-seat attack helicopter.

Power Plant: Two 1,536 shp General Electric T700-GE-700 turboshafts.

Performance: Max. speed, 191 mph (307 km/h); cruise, 179 mph (288 km/h); max. inclined climb, 3,200 ft/min (16,27 m/sec); hovering ceiling (in ground effect), 14,600 ft (4 453 m), (outside ground effect), 11,800 ft (3 600 m); service ceiling, 8,000 ft (2 440 m); max. range, 424 mls (682 km).

Weights: Empty, 9,900 lb (4 490 kg); primary mission, 13,600 lb (6 169 kg); max. take-off, 17,400 lb (7 892 kg).

Dimensions: Rotor diam, 48 ft 0 in (14,63 m); fuselage length, 49 ft 4½ in (15,05 m).

Notes: Winning contender in the US Army's AAH (Advanced Attack Helicopter) contest, the YAH-64 flew for the first time on September 30, 1975. Two prototypes were used for the initial trials and three more with fully integrated weapons systems are under construction and scheduled to commence trials in first half of 1979, planned total procurement comprising 536 AH-64s. The AH-64 is armed with a single-barrel 30-mm gun based on the chain-driven bolt system and suspended beneath the forward fuselage, and eight BGM-71A TOW anti-armour missiles may be carried, alternative armament including 16 Hellfire laser-seeking missiles. Target acquisition and designation and a pilot's night vision systems will be used.

KAMOV KA-25 (HORMONE A)

Country of Origin: USSR.
Type: Shipboard anti-submarine warfare helicopter.
Power Plant: Two 900 shp Glushenkov GTD-3 turboshafts.
Performance: (Estimated) Max. speed, 130 mph (209 km/h); normal cruise, 120 mph (193 km/h); max. range, 400 mls (644 km); service ceiling, 11,000 ft (3 353 m).
Weights: (Estimated) Empty, 10,500 lb (4 765 kg); max. take-off, 16,500 lb (7 484 kg).
Dimensions: Rotor diam (each), 51 ft 7½ in (15,74 m); approx. fuselage length, 35 ft 6 in (10,82 m).
Notes: Possessing a basically similar airframe to that of the Ka-25K (see 1973 edition) and employing a similar self-contained assembly comprising rotors, transmission, engines and auxiliaries, the Ka-25 serves with the Soviet Navy primarily in the ASW role but is also employed in the utility and transport roles. The ASW Ka-25 serves aboard the helicopter cruisers *Moskva* and *Leningrad*, and the carrier *Kiev*, as well as with shore-based units. A search radar installation is mounted in a nose radome, but other sensor housings and antennae differ widely from helicopter to helicopter. There is no evidence that externally-mounted weapons may be carried. Each landing wheel is surrounded by an inflatable pontoon surmounted by inflation bottles. The Hormone-A is intended for ASW operations whereas the Hormone-B is used for over-the-horizon missile targeting.

MBB BO 105CB

Country of Origin: Federal Germany.
Type: Five/six-seat light utility helicopter.
Power Plant: Two 420 shp Allison 250-C20B turboshafts.
Performance: Max. cruise, 152 mph (245 km/h) at sea level;
max. inclined climb, 1,771 ft/min (9,0 m/sec); hovering ceiling
(in ground effect), 9,514 ft (2 900 m); normal range, 388 mls
(625 km) at 5,000 ft (1 525 m).
Weights: Empty, 2,360 lb (1 070 kg); max. take-off, 5,070
lb (2 300 kg).
Dimensions: Rotor diam, 32 ft 1¾ in (9,80 m); fuselage
length, 28 ft 0½ in (8,55 m).
Notes: The BO 105, of which more than 450 examples had
been delivered by the beginning of 1979, features a rigid un-
articulated main rotor and production deliveries commenced
in 1971, the current commercial version being described above,
this having an uprated engine by comparison with the BO 105C
(see 1977 edition). The Federal German Army is to receive 227
BO 105M/VBH helicopters for liaison and observation tasks
and 212 BO 105A/PAH anti-armour helicopters equipped with
HOT missiles. Deliveries to the Army commence in September
1979 and will be completed by October 1982. Production rate
of the BO 105 at the beginning of 1979 was six—eight monthly,
increasing to 12—15 monthly during the year. Assembly is
undertaken in the Philippines and Indonesia (about 40 in
former and 60 in latter by 1979).

MBB-KAWASAKI BK 117

Countries of Origin: Federal Germany and Japan.

Type: Multi-purpose eight-to-ten-seat helicopter.

Power Plant: Two 600 shp Avco Lycoming LTS 101-650B-1 turboshafts.

Performance: (Estimated) Max. speed, 164 mph (264 km/h) at sea level; max. climb, 2,065 ft/min (10,49 m/sec); hovering ceiling (in ground effect), 14,775 ft (4 500 m), (out of ground effect, 12,475 ft (3 800 m); normal range, 342 mls (550 km).

Weights: Empty, 2,970 lb (1 347 kg); max. take-off, 6,170 lb (3 000 kg).

Dimensions: Rotor diam, 36 ft 1 in (11,00 m); fuselage length, 32 ft 5 in (9,88 m).

Notes: A co-operative development between Messerschmitt-Bölkow-Blohm of Federal Germany and Kawasaki of Japan, the first of two flying prototypes (P-2) is scheduled to fly in May 1979 at Ottobrun, with a second (P-2) following at Gifu in June 1979. The first pre-production helicopter (S-1) will fly mid-1980, with production deliveries scheduled to commence mid-1981. MBB is responsible for the main and tail rotor systems, tail unit and hydraulic components, while Kawasaki is responsible for production of the fuselage, undercarriage, transmission and some other components. Both military and civil versions are currently foreseen.

MIL MI-14 (HAZE-A)

Country of Origin: USSR.
Type: Amphibious anti-submarine helicopter.
Power Plant: Two 1,500 shp Isotov TV-2 turboshafts.
Performance: (Estimated) Max. speed, 143 mph (230 km/h); max. cruise, 130 mph (210 km/h); hovering ceiling (in ground effect), 5,250 ft (1 600 m), (out of ground effect), 2,295 ft (700 m); tactical radius, 124 mls (200 km).
Weights: (Estimated) Max. take-off, 26,455 lb (12 000 kg).
Dimensions: Rotor diam, 69 ft 10¼ in (21,29 m); fuselage length, 59 ft 7 in (18,15 m).
Notes: The Mi-14 amphibious anti-submarine warfare helicopter, which serves with shore-based elements of the Soviet Naval Air Force, is a derivative of the Mi-8 (see 1978 Edition) with essentially similar power plant and dynamic components, and much of the structure is common between the two helicopters. New features include the boat-type hull, outriggers which, housing the retractable lateral twin-wheel undercarriage members, incorporate water rudders, a search radar installation beneath the nose and a sonar "bird" beneath the tailboom root. The Mi-14 may presumably be used for over-the-horizon missile targeting and for such tasks as search and rescue. It may also be assumed that the Mi-14 possesses a weapons bay for ASW torpedoes, nuclear depth charges and other stores. This amphibious helicopter reportedly entered service in 1975.

MIL MI-24 (HIND-D)

Country of Origin: USSR.
Type: Assault and anti-armour helicopter.
Power Plant: Two 1,500 shp Isotov TV-2 turboshafts.
Performance: (Estimated) Max. speed, 160 mph (257 km/h); max. cruise, 140 mph (225 km/h); hovering ceiling (in ground effect), 6,000 ft (1 830 m), (out of ground effect), 1,600 ft (790 m); normal range, 300 mls (480 km).
Weights: Normal take-off, 22,000 lb (10 000 kg).
Dimensions: Rotor diam, 55 ft 0 in (16,76 m); fuselage length, 55 ft 6 in (16,90 m).
Notes: The Hind-D version of the Mi-24 assault helicopter embodies a redesigned forward fuselage and is optimised for the gunship role and has tandem stations for the weapons operator (in the extreme nose) and pilot with individual canopies, the cockpit of the latter being raised to afford an unobstructed forward view. A four-barrel Gatling-type large-calibre machine gun is mounted in an offset chin turret, there are four wing pylons for rocket pods (32×55-mm) and end-plate pylons at the wingtips carry rails for four Swatter anti-tank missiles. Apart from the Hind-D, the principal service versions of the Mi-24 are the Hind-A (see 1977 edition) armed assault helicopter featuring a flight deck for a crew of four, and the essentially similar Hind-C which has no nose gun and undernose sighting system, or missile rails at wingtips. The Hind-C and Hind-D are apparently complementary.

SIKORSKY S-61D (SEA KING)

Country of Origin: USA.

Type: Amphibious anti-submarine helicopter.

Power Plant: Two 1,500 shp General Electric T58-GE-10 turboshafts.

Performance: Max. speed, 172 mph (277 km/h) at sea level; inclined climb, 2,200 ft/min (11,2 m/sec); hovering ceiling (out of ground effect), 8,200 ft (2 500 m); range (with 10% reserves), 622 mls (1 000 km).

Weights: Empty equipped, 12,087 lb (5 481 kg); max. take-off, 20,500 lb (9 297 kg).

Dimensions: Rotor diam, 62 ft 0 in (18,90 m); fuselage length, 54 ft 9 in (16,69 m).

Notes: A more powerful derivative of the S-61B, the S-61D serves with the US Navy as the SH-3D (illustrated above), 72 helicopters of this type following on production of 255 SH-3As (S-61Bs) for the ASW role for the US Navy, four being supplied to the Brazilian Navy and 22 to the Spanish Navy. Four similar aircraft have been supplied to the Argentine Navy as S-61D-4s and 11 have been supplied to the US Army/US Marine Corps Executive Flight Detachment as VH-3Ds. Licence manufacture of the S-61D is being undertaken in the United Kingdom (see pages 248–9), in Japan for the Maritime Self-Defence Force and in Italy by Agusta for the Italian and Iranian navies. The SH-3G and SH-3H are upgraded conversions of the SH-3A.

SIKORSKY S-61R

Country of Origin: USA.
Type: Amphibious transport and rescue helicopter.
Power Plant: (CH-3E) Two 1,500 shp General Electric T58-GE-5 turboshafts.
Performance: (CH-3E at 21,247 lb/9 635 kg) Max. speed, 162 mph (261 km/h) at sea level; range cruise, 144 mph (232 km/h); max. inclined climb, 1,310 ft/min (6,6 m/sec); hovering ceiling (in ground effect), 4,100 ft (1 250 m); range with 10% reserves, 465 mls (748 km).
Weights: (CH-3E) Empty, 13,255 lb (6 010 kg); normal take-off, 21,247 lb (9 635 kg); max. take-off, 22,050 lb (10 000 kg).
Dimensions: Rotor diam, 62 ft 0 in (18,90 m); fuselage length, 57 ft 3 in (17,45 m).
Notes: Although based on the S-61A, the S-61R embodies numerous design changes, including a rear ramp and a tricycle-type undercarriage. Initial model for the USAF was the CH-3C with 1,300 shp T58-GE-1 turboshafts, but this was subsequently updated to CH-3E standards. The CH-3E can accommodate 25–30 troops or 5,000 lb (2 270 kg) of cargo, and may be fitted with a TAT-102 barbette on each sponson mounting a 7,62-mm Minigun. The HH-3E is a USAF rescue version with armour, self-sealing tanks, and refuelling probe, and the HH-3F Pelican (illustrated) is a US Coast Guard search and rescue model. Licence manufacture is undertaken by Agusta in Italy.

SIKORSKY CH-53E SUPER STALLION

Country of Origin: USA.
Type: Amphibious assault transport helicopter.
Power Plant: Three 4,380 shp General Electric T64-GE-415 turboshafts.
Performance: Max. speed, 196 mph (315 km/h) at sea level; max. cruise, 173 mph (278 km/h).
Weights: Operational empty, 33,000 lb (14 968 kg); max. take-off, 69,750 lb (31 638 kg).
Dimensions: Rotor diam., 79 ft 0 in (24,08 m); fuselage length, 73 ft 5 in (22,38 m).
Notes: The CH-53E is a growth version of the CH-53D Sea Stallion (see 1974 edition) embodying a third engine, an uprated transmission system, a seventh main rotor blade and increased rotor diameter. The first of two prototypes was flown on March 1, 1974, and the first of two pre-production prototypes flew on December 8, 1975, a production order being placed in the spring of 1978. The CH-53E can accommodate up to 56 troops in a high-density arrangement and can lift a 32,000-lb (14 515-kg) external load over a radius of 58 miles (93 km) at sea level in a 90 deg F temperature. The planned production programme envisages the acquisition from May 1980 of 49 helicopters of this type divided between the US Navy (16) and US Marine Corps (33). The CH-53E offers a major performance advance and can retrieve 93 per cent of USMC tactical aircraft without disassembly.

SIKORSKY S-70 (UH-60A) BLACK HAWK

Country of Origin: USA.

Type: Tactical transport helicopter.

Power Plant: Two 1,543 shp General Election T700-GE-700 turboshafts.

Performance: Max. speed, 224 mph (360 km/h) at sea level; cruise, 166 mph (267 km/h); vertical climb rate, 450 ft/min (2,28 m/sec); hovering ceiling (in ground effect), 10,000 ft (3 048 m), (out of ground effect), 5,800 ft (1 758 m); endurance 2·3–3·0 hrs.

Weights: Design gross, 16,500 lb (7 485 kg); max. take-off, 22,000 lb (9 979 kg).

Dimensions: Rotor diam, 53 ft 8 in (16,23 m); fuselage length, 50 ft 0¾ in (15,26 m).

Notes: The Black Hawk was winner of the US Army's UTTAS (Utility Tactical Transport Aircraft System) contest, and contracts had been announced by beginning of 1979 for 200 examples with deliveries having commenced September 1978. The first of three YUH-60As was flown on October 17, 1974, and a company-funded forth prototype flew on May 23, 1975. The Black Hawk is primarily a combat assault squad carrier, accommodating 11 fully-equipped troops, but it is capable of carrying an 8,000-lb (3 629-kg) slung load and can perform a variety of secondary missions, such as reconnaissance and troop resupply. Commercial versions of the Black Hawk were under study at the beginning of 1978.

SIKORSKY S-70L (SH-60B)

Country of Origin: USA.

Type: Shipboard multi-role helicopter.

Power Plant: Two 1,630 shp General Electric T700-GE-400 turboshafts.

Performance: (Estimated) Max. cruise, 172 mph (277 km/h); max. vertical climb rate, 450 ft/min (2,28 m/sec); ceiling, 10,000 ft (3 050 m); time on station (at radius of 57 mls/92 km), 3 hrs, (at radius of 173 mls/278 km), 1 hr.

Weights: Mission loaded (ASW), 19,377 lb (8 789 kg), (anti-ship surveillance), 17,605 lb (7 985 kg).

Dimensions: Rotor diam, 53 ft 8 in (16,36 m); fuselage length, 50 ft 0¾ in (15,26 m).

Notes: The S-70L was selected by the US Navy on September 1, 1977, as winning contender in its LAMPS (Light Airborne Multi-purpose System) Mk. III helicopter, the first of five prototypes having been scheduled to fly in the first quarter of 1979, and the US Navy having a requirement for more than 200 helicopters of this type with deliveries commencing in 1981 under the designation SH-60B. The S-70L is a derivative of the UH-60A Black Hawk and will be capable of carrying two homing torpedoes, 25 sonobuoys and an extensive range of avionics. It will serve aboard DD-963 destroyers, DDG-47 Aegis cruisers and FFG-7 guided-missile frigates as an integral extension of the sensor and weapons system of the launching vessel.

SIKORSKY S-76

County of Origin: USA.
Type: Fourteen-seat commercial transport helicopter.
Power Plant: Two 700 shp Allison 250-C30 turboshafts.
Performance: Max. speed, 179 mph (288 km/h); max. cruise, 167 mph (268 km/h); range cruise, 145 mph (233 km/h); hovering ceiling (in ground effect), 5,100 ft (1 524 m), (out of ground effect), 1,400 ft (427 m); range (full payload and 30 min reserve), 460 mls (740 km).
Weights: Empty, 4,942 lb (2 241 kg); max. take-off, 9,700 lb (4 399 kg).
Dimensions: Rotor diam, 44 ft 0 in (13,41 m); fuselage length, 44 ft 1 in (13,44 m).
Notes: The first of four prototypes of the S-76 flew on March 13, 1977, and customer deliveries commenced early 1979, eight having been completed by end of 1978 with a production rate of seven per month being attained by March 1979. The S-76 is unique among Sikorsky commercial helicopters in that conceptually it owes nothing to an existing military model, although it has been designed to conform with appropriate military specifications and military customers were included among contracts for some 200 helicopters of this type that had been ordered by the beginning of 1979, with 70–80 to be delivered during year. The S-76 may be fitted with extended-range tanks, cargo hook and rescue hoist, and a version has been proposed to the US Coast Guard.

WESTLAND SEA KING MK. 2

Country of Origin: United Kingdom (US licence).
Type: Anti-submarine warfare and search-and-rescue heli-copter.
Power Plant: Two 1,500 shp Rolls-Royce Gnome 1400-1 turboshafts.
Performance: Max. speed, 143 mph (230 km/h); max. con-tinuous cruise at sea level, 131 mph (211 km/h); hovering ceil-ing (in ground effect), 5,000 ft (1 525 m), (out of ground effect), 3,200 ft (975 m); range (standard fuel), 764 mls (1 230 km), (auxiliary fuel), 937 mls (1 507 km).
Weights: Empty equipped (ASW), 13,672 lb (6 201 kg), (SAR), 12,376 lb (5 613 kg); max. take-off, 21,000 lb (9 525 kg).
Dimensions: Rotor diam., 62 ft 0 in (18,90 m); fuselage length, 55 ft 9¾ in (17,01 m).
Notes: The Sea King Mk 2 is an uprated version of the basic ASW and SAR derivative of the licence-built S-61D (see page 242), the first Mk 2 being flown on June 30, 1974, and being one of 10 Sea King Mk 50s ordered by the Australian Navy. Twenty-one have been ordered for the Royal Navy as Sea King HAS Mk 2s and 15 examples of a SAR version (illustrated above) have been ordered by the RAF as Sea King HAR Mk 3s, these having begun to enter service during the first half of 1978. A total of 213 Westland-built derivatives of the S-61D (includ-ing Commandos) had been ordered by the beginning of 1979.

WESTLAND COMMANDO MK. 2

Country of Origin: United Kingdom (US licence).
Type: Tactical transport helicopter.
Power Plant: Two 1,590 shp Rolls-Royce Gnome 1400-1 turboshafts.
Performance: Max. speed (at 19,900 lb/9 046 kg), 138 mph (222 km/h); max. cruise, 127 mph (204 km/h); max. inclined climb, 1,930 ft/min (9,8 m/sec); range (with 30 troops), 161 mls (259 km); ferry range, 1,036 mls (1 668 km).
Weights: Empty equipped, 11,487–12,122 lb (5 221–5 510 kg); max. take-off, 20,000 lb (9 072 kg).
Dimensions: Rotor diam, 62 ft 0 in (18,89 m); fuselage length, 54 ft 9 in (16,69 m).
Notes: The Commando is a Westland-developed land-based army support helicopter derivative of the licence-built Sikorsky S-61D Sea King (see page 242), search radar and other specialised items being deleted together with the sponsons which endow the Sea King with amphibious capability. The first five examples completed as Commando Mk. 1s were minimum change conversions of Sea King airframes, the first of these flying on September 12, 1973, but subsequent Commandos are being built to Mk. 2 standards with the uprated Gnome turboshafts selected for the Sea King Mk. 50s ordered by Australia. The first production deliveries (to Egypt) commenced in 1975, that illustrated being one of four for Qatar, and 15 are on order for the Royal Marines.

WESTLAND WG.13 LYNX

Country of Origin: United Kingdom.
Type: Multi-purpose, ASW and transport helicopter.
Power Plant: Two 900 shp Rolls-Royce BS.360-07-26 Gem 100 turboshafts.
Performance: Max. speed, 207 mph (333 km/h); max. continuous sea level cruise, 170 mph (273 km/h); max. inclined climb, 1,174 ft/min (11,05 m/sec); hovering ceiling (out of ground effect), 12,000 ft (3 660 m); max. range (internal fuel), 391 mls (629 km); max. ferry range (auxiliary fuel), 787 mls (1 266 km).
Weights: (HAS Mk 2) Operational empty, 6,767–6,999 lb (3 069–3 174 kg); max. take-off, 9,500 lb (4 309 kg).
Dimensions: Rotor diam, 42 ft 0 in (12,80 m); fuselage length, 39 ft 1¼ in (11,92 m).
Notes: The first of 13 development Lynxes was flown on March 21, 1971, with the first production example (an HAS Mk 2) flying on February 10, 1976. By the beginning of 1979, production rate was nine per month and 285 were on order, including 26 for the French Navy, 60 for the Royal Navy, 100 for the British Army, seven for the Danish Navy, nine for the Brazilian Navy, four for Norway and 16 for the Netherlands Navy. The Lynx AH Mk 1 is the British Army's general utility version and the Lynx HAS Mk 2 is the ASW version for the Royal Navy. Licence manufacture (of some 230) is to be undertaken in Egypt.

ACKNOWLEDGEMENTS

The author wishes to record his thanks to the following sources of copyright photographs appearing in this volume: Aviation Magazine International, page 154; Flug Revue International, pages 158 and 194; A. Klomp, page 156; R. H. Judges, page 172; Dave Thomas, page 188; Stephen Peltz, pages 124 and 238; Swedish Air Force, pages 192, 128 and 206. The three-view silhouette drawings published in this volume are copyright Pilot Press Limited and may not be reproduced without prior permission.

INDEX OF AIRCRAFT TYPES

Printed for the Publishers by
Butler & Tanner Ltd, Frome and London

0079 · 1178